AF439079

Biblical Wealth and Prosperity:
A Christian Guide to Manifesting Money

P.B. Lamb

ISBN: 979-8-8689-2543-6 (sc)

ISBN: 979-8-8689-2544-3 (e)

Dedication:

This book is dedicated to God first, my husband and all my children without whom my life would be incomplete! And finally, to all the lost people out there seeking answers but failing to find them - this book is for you!

Table of Contents

Introduction

Prosperity, in the Christian perspective, is not just about material wealth; it is about embracing a life filled with success, abundance, and well-being on all fronts. It is the kind of prosperity that goes beyond the tangible and touches every aspect of your existence.

For Christians, this holistic well-being involves not only financial abundance but also spiritual, emotional, and physical health. It is a state of being where every part of your life is in harmony, and you feel truly blessed.

This blessing is believed to come from faith in God and a commitment to living in alignment with biblical principles. The idea of "manifestation," as used in the title of the book, is all about making the unseen become seen.

It is a concept meant to teach Christians how to harness these techniques to build wealth in a way that serves God and benefits one another. In essence, it is about using your faith and principles to create a better life for yourself and those around you, both spiritually and materially.

Christian prosperity is a multifaceted concept deeply embedded in faith and a commitment to living in harmony with God's divine will. Its core components encompass spiritual fulfillment, rooted in a deep connection with God through faith in Jesus, ongoing spiritual growth, and unwavering trust in divine guidance.

Moral and ethical integrity underpins this prosperity, emphasizing principles of honesty, integrity, and ethical conduct in all facets of life. Financial abundance, while part of the equation, is seen as a means to serve God and others rather than an end in itself, with wealth regarded as a resource to be responsibly managed for the betterment of society.

Health and well-being highlight the sacred nature of one's body and mind, emphasizing diligent self-care. Generosity and service form integral parts of Christian prosperity, with the call to provide for those in need, support charitable causes, and actively engage in community service.

Contentment and gratitude replace ceaseless desire with an enduring sense of sufficiency and thankfulness for God's provision.

Purpose and calling, central to Christian prosperity, involve living a purpose-driven life, recognizing one's divine calling, and using one's talents and resources to fulfill God's overarching plan.

These principles collectively shape a holistic form of prosperity grounded in faith, ethical conduct, selflessness, gratitude, and divine purpose, placing God at its core, and reflecting the values and teachings of Christianity.

It is important to note that Christian prosperity interpretations can vary among denominations and individuals within the Christian faith.

While some emphasize material wealth as a sign of God's favor, others focus more on spiritual and moral well-being as indicators of true prosperity.

Abundance through Christian principles often refers to achieving wealth and success while adhering to Christian values and beliefs.

This book will focus on the following fundamental values from a Christian perspective that can contribute to abundance: *Faith, Stewardship, Generosity, Integrity, Service, Gratitude, Hard Work, Contentment, Prayer, and Community.*

> *Faith:* Trust in God's providence and believe He will provide for your needs as you work diligently.
> *Stewardship:* Managing resources wisely and responsibly, recognizing that everything belongs to God.
> *Generosity:* Giving to others in need, practicing charity, and sharing your blessings with those less fortunate.
> *Integrity:* Conducting business and life with honesty, ethics, and moral values.

Service: Serving others selflessly and with a servant's heart, as Jesus Christ exemplifies.

Gratitude: Cultivating a spirit of thankfulness for what you have rather than constantly desiring more.

Hard Work: Diligently applying your skills and efforts to achieve success, guided by the belief that work is a form of worship.

Contentment: Finding peace and satisfaction in your current circumstances while aspiring for growth.

Prayer: Seeking guidance, wisdom, and strength through prayer and a personal relationship with God.

Community: Building supportive relationships with fellow Christians and contributing to the well-being of your community.

These principles can be integrated into various aspects of life, including personal finances, business, and relationships, to pursue abundance while staying true to Christian values.

It is essential to seek guidance from Christian leaders and mentors and reflect on how these principles align with your goals and actions. In this book, I will show you biblically how to be Prosperous and use your abundance for the Kingdom that God has called us to be a part of.

I am committed to maintaining a strong connection to Bible teachings and verses. This choice is deliberate, ensuring that the authority in these words is not solely mine but is rooted in the word and authority of God. Further, I will show how to manifest wealth for God.

Yes, I specifically use the word 'manifest,' and while some people believe the word to be aligned only with Enlightenment and more specifically with the Law of Attraction, which carries the spiritual connotations of enlightenment, it is Biblical.

However, this book will show you that the principles of the 'Law of Attraction' are, in fact, biblical, not a new-age philosophy.

God calls upon us to create wealth for His Kingdom.

"All Scripture is inspired by God and profitable for teaching, for reproof, for correction, for training in righteousness; so that the man of God may be adequate, equipped for every good work," 2 Timothy 3:16-17 NASB.

Chapter 1: Understanding Biblical Perspectives on Wealth

In the Bible, there is a profound message about money, wealth, and possessions, but let us dive into the heart of it, starting with something deeply personal – faith.

Now, I am not referring to the fundamental faith in God that likely brought you here. It is about something more specific – it is about believing in prosperity through your unwavering faith in God. It is the kind of faith that goes beyond just acknowledging God's existence; it is about trusting that God wants you to thrive, not just survive.

It is believing that your faith can lead to abundance in every aspect of your life, including your finances. This faith is the cornerstone, the driving force that can shape your journey towards prosperity, and it is a crucial theme we will explore in this chapter.

It is about understanding that God's plan for you is not just about getting by but about living a life filled with abundance, all while staying true to the principles and teachings of the Bible.

Faith

When I was a child, I heard the words "you just have to believe," and "you need to just have faith," but not one person ever actually defined faith for me. I was just expected to believe, like we all believed in Santa Claus, simply because I was told to believe.

Except believing in Santa Claus was easy as a child because there was a tangible proof of his existence at the end of the Thanksgiving parade, in the mall during the month of December, and on Christmas morning when I ran into the living room to find all the toys, he had left for me.

Having faith in God, especially in His provision and trusting in Him seemed to be a much different type of faith. Faith in God's provision involves trusting in God's ability and willingness to provide for your needs. This trust can alleviate worry about financial matters and foster a sense of security.

Many Christians believe that through prayer and faith, they can seek God's guidance and blessings in their financial endeavors. This might include praying to meet financial needs or wisdom in economic decisions.

Luke 18:27 NASB reminds us, *"The things that are impossible with people are possible with God."*

Philippians 4:12 NASB says,

"I know how to get along with humble means, and I also know how to live in prosperity; in any and every circumstance I have learned the secret of being filled and going hungry, both of having abundance and suffering need."

Having a faith like this can truly transform your outlook on life, infusing it with positivity and hope, qualities that are like fertile soil for financial success to take root and thrive.

This faith becomes the driving force that inspires you to work diligently, even when faced with financial challenges. It is the unwavering belief that your efforts are part of a greater plan for your prosperity.

What is beautiful is that this faith often leads to acts of generosity and charity. By giving to others and supporting those in need, you not only make a positive impact on their lives but also find a profound sense of fulfillment and blessings in return.

It is a cycle of abundance that starts with your faith in God and extends to your fellow human beings.

Throughout this book, you will come across references to many Bible verses and texts that offer timeless wisdom on managing finances, dealing with debt, and making sound investments. Your faith acts as a guiding light, leading you to apply these principles to your financial decisions.

It is important to note that the role of faith in financial blessings is a matter of personal belief and interpretation. Some see strong faith as a direct path to financial prosperity, while others view it as a source of inner peace, resilience, and ethical guidance in financial matters.

Regardless of your perspective, it is vital to approach financial decisions with prudence and responsibility while seeking guidance from God. Your faith can guide you, but your actions and choices are still yours to make, always with the wisdom of faith as your companion.

Stewardship

Through Stewardship, Christians are called to be good stewards of the resources entrusted to them. The Parable of the Talents (Matthew 25:14-30 NASB) illustrates the importance of wisely using one's talents and resources.

"For it is just like a man about to go on a journey, who called his own slaves and entrusted his possessions to them. To one he gave five talents, to another two, and to another, one, each according to his own ability; and he went on his journey. Immediately the one who received the five talents went and traded with them and gained five more talents. In the same manner the one who had received the two talents gained two more. But he who received the one talent went away and dug a hole

in the ground and hid his master's money. Now after a long time the master of those slaves came and settled accounts with them. The one who had received the five talents came up and brought five more talents, saying 'Master, you entrusted five talents to me. See, I have gained five more talents.' His master said to him, 'Well done, good and faithful slave. You were faithful with a few things; I will put you in charge of many things; enter into the joy of your master.'

Also the one who had received the two talents came up and said, 'Master, you entrusted two talents to me. See, I have gained two more talents.' His master said to him, 'Well done, good and faithful slave. You were faithful with a few things; I will put you in charge of many things; enter into the joy of your master.'

And the one also who had received the one talent came up and said, 'Master, I knew you to a hard man, reaping where you did not sow and gathering where you scattered no seed. And I was afraid and went away and hid your talent in the ground. See, you have what is yours.'
But his master answered and said to him, 'You wicked, lazy slave, you knew that I reap where I did not sow and gather where I scattered no seed. Then you ought to have put my money in the bank, and on my arrival I would have received my money back with interest. Therefore take away the talent from him, and give it to the one who has the then talents.'

For to everyone who has, more shall be given, and he will have an abundance; but from the one who does not have, even what he does have shall be taken away. Throw out the worthless slave into the outer darkness; in that place there will be weeping and gnashing of teeth."

In this parable, Jesus tells the disciples to use their God-given gifts for the service of God and to take risks for the sake of the Kingdom of God. Do not hide your 'talents' or your 'money' or 'wealth;' instead, use them for the Kingdom of God, and God will reward those who better their lives and those in their communities.

Do not bury your talents or riches, waiting for your own personal gains and salvation; instead, be a good steward of God's abundance by finding ways to grow and improve it for His Kingdom.

The Bible teaches that contentment should be found in Godliness rather than wealth.

Hebrews 13:5 NIV says, *"Keep your lives free from the love of money and be content with what you have, because God has said, 'Never will I leave you; never will I forsake you.'"*

Here is where you need to understand the relationship between money and Christianity. Wealth and being wealthy are not the cause of evil. It is the love of money above all things that is the root cause.

Money, by itself, is not evil. It is a tool, something to trade for items and services. But the love of money, or the pursuit of money above our pursuit of the love from God, that is where you find strife and woes.

In Matthew 6:24 NIV, Jesus says, *"No one can serve two masters. Either you will hate the one and love the other, or you will be devoted to the one and despise the other. You can't serve both God and money."*

This underscores the need to prioritize God over wealth.

I want to point out that the Bible does mention 'get rich' schemes in a way it warns of falling into temptation and traps. (See Matthew 6:24 above) Do not be so blinded by the number of dollars and the promises of wealth that you fall into traps.

Some entities, loosely labeled as companies, exploit the sacred name of Jesus and the concept of 'Kingdom Building' to peddle assurances of prosperity and affluence.

As a business proprietor, should you choose to frame your enterprise around the noble pursuit of advancing God's Kingdom, it is imperative that your core values, principles, and operational strategies align with this sacred mission, rather than being driven solely by promises of worldly riches.

To embody the essence of Kingdom Building, prioritize stewardship of your financial resources and exercise discernment in allocating your worldly assets for the betterment of God's Kingdom.

True contentment lies not in the pursuit of earthly wealth but in the conscientious and principled use of resources to serve a higher purpose. As you navigate the realm of business, let the foundations of your enterprise be rooted in genuine commitment to God's Kingdom, transcending the allure of mere material gain.

I did not mention tithing to your church, religious establishment, or any other prosperity theology that has been overused since the 1950s. That is because there is a different message that needs to be heard at this time. Which is – God wants you to use your wealth, abundance, prosperity, and money to build His Kingdom.

It is not about the guilt associated with not giving to the church or you will be punished and struck down from your place in the Kingdom of God.

No, God calls us, as good stewards, to return our money and wealth to the Kingdom. If, for you, that means you tithe every Sunday and take ten percent of all your earnings, then give it to your church, that is your financial purpose and calling.

However, many have a calling to give to people experiencing poverty, take care of people experiencing homelessness, or give in some other way. God never said you must give to the church and *only the church* as the only way into heaven.

You may need to reread that sentence until you truly understand it.

I pray you stop judging one another based on what is given in the four walls of the church and realize that generosity to the community and helping others are other forms of giving back to God's Kingdom. This book will cover this topic in depth in Chapter Four.

Generosity

The Bible consistently emphasizes the virtue of generosity. In 2 Corinthians 9:6-7 NASB, it is stated, *"The point is this: whoever sows sparingly will also reap sparingly, and whoever sows bountifully will also reap bountifully. Each one must give as he has decided in his heart, not reluctantly or under compulsion, for God loves a cheerful giver."*

Further insight can be gained by exploring 1 Timothy 6:17-18 NASB, which advises, *"Instruct those who are rich in this present world not to be conceited or to set their hope on the uncertainty of riches, but on God, who richly supplies us with all things to enjoy. Instruct them to do good, to be rich in good works, to be generous and ready to share, storing up for themselves the treasure of a good foundation for the future, so that they may take hold of that which is truly life."*

This underscores the idea that true wealth is found in a generosity of spirit and actions, rather than in the mere accumulation of riches.

In the context of our contemporary society (in 2023), it can be challenging to overcome the instinctive hesitation to part with our financial resources. We have been systematically conditioned to fear that giving away money will result in personal lack.

This, however, is a misconception.

The world is abundant with financial resources. Have you ever had a twenty-dollar bill or just a few ones in your wallet and you saw a homeless person begging, but your first thought was, 'If I give this to them, then I won't have the cash I need for…' or 'they do not need this they are just going to use this for drugs/alcohol/etc.'

Here, I challenge you to be more like Jesus Christ in your thinking, aligning you with God's prosperity. Instead of "I won't have it for……" change your thinking to "I bless this money as I send it out," knowing it will come back to you.

Do not judge the person asking because you do not know the plans of God. That person may buy a pack of cigarettes, soda, or sandwiches at a small mom-and-pop store that needs the sale to stay in business one more day.

The Bible warns not to judge anyway. *"Do not judge so that you will not be judged,"* Matthew 7:1 NASB.

The result of that dollar bill, no matter the denomination of the bill, is in God's hands, not our personal judgment.

The Bible frequently emphasizes caring for the poor and needy. There are over one hundred verses in the Bible that speak of giving and receiving.

But the one I love the most is Proverbs 19:17 NASB, *"One who is gracious to a poor man lends to the Lord, And He will repay him for his good deed."*

God will reward you for putting your faith in His plan for the money, not your judgment of the situation, especially if you give from the heart.

I want to caution here, though, while the Bible encourages generosity and promises blessings for those who give, it does not guarantee immediate financial prosperity in return for charitable acts.

Therefore, do not give with the thought, "If I give this, then God will bless me back ten times."

That is false thinking and not a place of genuine kindness or cheerful giving; it is selfish. Blessings can take various forms, including spiritual and emotional well-being.

Proverbs 11:25 NIV says, *"A generous person will prosper; whoever refreshes others will be refreshed."*

Proper Attitude

I remember when I was a young mother in my early twenties, just starting out on my own with a family to support. The financial pressure was immense, with expenses piling up for diapers, formula, and baby wipes, all of which came at a high cost. I did not have any extra money to spare, and my financial situation was far from comfortable.

It was during this time that I attended a church that strongly emphasized the importance of tithing, contributing ten percent of your gross earnings every Sunday. The church's message carried a sense of guilt, making it even more challenging for me given my tight finances.

Then there was another instance in my life when I had pledged a certain amount of my income to a church, but a series of unexpected and life-altering events left me in an even tighter financial spot.

To my shock and dismay, I received a collection notice from the very same church I had pledged to support. This was a low point in my life when I had more debt than income, and the experience left a bitter taste in my mouth.

It was difficult for me to reconcile the teachings of faith, which emphasized the significance of giving, with the actions of the church that seemed more concerned with collecting money.

These experiences undoubtedly shaped my attitude toward money. They instilled in me a sense of resentment, not only towards financial institutions but also towards organized religion's approach to wealth.

Many of you reading this book may have experienced similar situations, where the church's teachings on money created a sense of negativity, conflict, and even disillusionment.

These types of incidents are just the tip of the iceberg when it comes to the complex relationship between faith, money, and social issues tied to wealth and poverty. They illustrate how personal experiences can profoundly influence one's attitude toward money, often in ways that are difficult to shake off.

In retrospect, these challenges have led me to seek a more balanced and compassionate perspective on money, one that goes beyond guilt and collection notices.

All those feelings on money aside, the Bible instructs that you are to love and support one another. The command of "Love one Another" appears in the New Testament eleven times.

Jesus himself said it three times, John 13:34-35 NIV *"A new command I give you: Love one another. As I have loved you, so you must love one another. By this everyone will know that you are my disciples if you love one another."*

How amazing it is that you will be known as His disciples if you love one another!

Talk about putting you in alignment with a proper attitude.

Additionally, it is important to reevaluate your approach to giving. If you give sparingly out of fear that you might not have enough, it can hinder your own prosperity and abundance.

Instead, you should cultivate a mindset that money is a tool, a resource that God provides to bless both yourself and others. This shift in perspective can lead to a more open-hearted and generous approach to finances.

You must also guard against valuing money above the love of God and your love for one another.

The Bible reminds you that the love of money can be a root of all kinds of evil, but it is not money itself that is the problem.

It is your attitude and intentions regarding money that matter most. By using money as a means to support others and to further the greater good, you can align your financial attitudes with your spiritual values.

It is also crucial not to hoard money out of fear of losing it or missing out. Trusting in God's guidance and provision means letting go of this fear and allowing money to flow, fulfilling its purpose as a tool for blessing others and yourself.

Indeed, the Bible carries a message of hope, faith, and trust in God's guidance and provision during challenging times.

So, relating this back to finances and prosperity, it is essential to reflect on these positive attitude principles and transform our mindset about money.

Changing your mindset about money involves developing a healthy, positive attitude towards finances, wealth, and generosity. It is about recognizing money as a tool for both personal and collective well-being and ensuring that love for one another and love for God always take precedence over the love of money.

This shift in perspective can lead to a more fulfilling and spiritually aligned relationship with wealth and prosperity.

Misconceptions

As I reflect on the fundamental principles about money and prosperity as outlined in the Bible, it is crucial to delve into some prevalent misconceptions surrounding Christianity and wealth.

Understanding these misconceptions can lead to a more nuanced and accurate interpretation of the biblical teachings on wealth and prosperity.

When I delved into the research for this specific chapter, I was motivated by the desire to shed light on common misconceptions that many of us may have encountered or even held.

These misconceptions can be subtle yet influential, potentially leading us to inadvertently push away the blessings God intends for us. I encourage you to consider how some of these thoughts and feelings may have resonated with you.

As you explore each misconception, take a moment to reflect and ask yourself if you have ever felt this way. Addressing and dispelling these misconceptions is essential because they can create mental barriers, hindering us from fully embracing the providence that God has in store for us.

1. *Wealth is Inherently Evil:* One common misconception is that the Bible condemns wealth as inherently evil. While the Bible does caution against the love of money *(1 Timothy 6:10 NIV: "For the love of money is a root of all kinds of evil…")* and the potential dangers of wealth, it does not declare wealth itself sinful.

The attitude and love of wealth lead to moral and spiritual issues. *(Matthew 6:24 NIV: "…You can't serve both God and money.")*

The phrase "Money is the root of all evil" is a common misquotation of the verse in 1 Timothy.

Money is simply a tool, just as a ruler is a tool for measuring things and a clock is a tool for telling time. Neither the ruler nor the clock is evil; they are just tools.

2. *Prosperity Gospel:* The basics of prosperity gospel teaches that faith in God will lead to financial prosperity and success. This view is controversial and not universally accepted within Christian theology.

The Bible does not guarantee material wealth directly from one's faith.

The teachings in prosperity gospel rely heavily on non-traditional interpretations of passages such as Malachi 3:10 KJV, *"Bring ye all the tithes into the storehouse, that there may be meat in mine house, and prove me now herewith, saith the Lord of hosts, if I will not open you the windows of heaven, and pour you out a blessing, that there shall not be room enough to receive it."*

The New American Standard Bible has a different translation of the same verse: *"Bring the whole tithe into the storehouse, so that there may be food in My house, and test Me now in this,"* says the Lord of hosts, *"if I will not open for you the windows of heaven and pour out for you a blessing until it overflows."*

The next verse, Malachi 3:11, continues with, *"Then I will rebuke the devourer for you, so that it will not destroy the fruits of the ground; nor will your vine in the field cast its grapes,'says the Lord of hosts."*

The interesting thing about this chapter and passage in Malachi is that it talks about not robbing God. It has nothing to do with giving your money to God to be blessed.

3. *Poverty Equals Righteousness:* Some people mistakenly believe poverty is a sign of righteousness and wealth is a sign of unrighteousness.

While the Bible does commend the virtues of humility and selflessness, it does not equate poverty with morality or wealth with unrighteousness. The idea of "poor in righteousness" stems from one of the teachings of Jesus in the New Testament.

Matthew 5:3 NIV, *"Blessed are the poor in spirit, for theirs is the kingdom of heaven."* Jesus is teaching about the qualities that lead to spiritual blessings. "Poor in spirit" refers to those who recognize their spiritual poverty or need for God and HIS righteousness. It is not a direct reference to being monetarily poor.

4. *Financial Success Guarantees God's Favor*: Assuming that financial success is a clear indicator of God's favor is another misconception.

The Bible teaches that God's favor is not solely measured by material wealth, and righteous individuals can face financial hardships. In Proverbs 3:3-4 NASB, it says, *"Do not let kindness and truth leave you; Bind them around your neck, Write them on the tablet of your heart. So you will find favor and good repute in the sight of God and man."*

The idea that financial success guarantees God's favor is a misconception in some religious and prosperity gospel teachings. It is important to note that this idea lacks a Scriptural Basis as the Bible does not equate financial success with God's favor.

Jesus taught and emphasized the importance of spiritual wealth, not material wealth.

5. *The Bible Promotes Capitalism or Socialism*: Some individuals use biblical principles to argue for or against specific economic systems like capitalism or socialism.

The Bible does not explicitly endorse any economic system but provides moral and ethical guidelines for how individuals should handle their resources within various economic contexts.

At the time of this book (2023), social, economic, and political injustice is rampant everywhere. But a lack of Biblical teachings has led to this, not the other way around. Here again, there are no scriptural references that argue this misconception.

As you reflect on the guidance found in the Bible regarding financial matters, consider the rich tapestry it offers—one woven with threads of faith, stewardship, generosity, and ethical conduct.

These timeless principles provide not just a roadmap for managing wealth but also a profound invitation to infuse your financial decisions with personal values that extend beyond mere material gain.

Embracing the wisdom within these pages can lead to a more fulfilling and purpose-driven approach to your financial journey, grounded in a connection between your beliefs and the way you manage your resources.

So, as you navigate the complexities of wealth, let the teachings of the Bible serve as a personal and meaningful guide for your financial choices and aspirations.

Chapter 2: Developing a Faith-Focused Mindset

In this section, my aim is to delve into the Christian faith, bearing in mind that the principles for nurturing a positive faith-centered mindset can be universally relevant, often crossing many religious boundaries.

When you begin to ponder your beliefs, values, and the significance of faith in your life, it is crucial to ask yourself why faith matters to you and why you are driven to nurture it.

This self-inquiry helps to understand your core convictions and principles. What are the foundational beliefs of your faith? What values hold utmost importance in your spiritual journey?

By delving into these questions, you can establish a firm bedrock for your positive faith-focused mindset. Having a positive faith-focused mindset is the bedrock to manifesting financial prosperity.

As you work throughout this journey, I encourage you to record your responses in a journal or a place where you can revisit them later for reflection and reaffirmation.

Regular prayer and meditation are powerful tools for establishing a profound connection with your faith. They serve as spaces for reflection, expressions of gratitude, and an opportunity to seek divine guidance from God.

These moments of contemplation can anchor you in your faith and help you navigate life's challenges – especially financial ones - with a strengthened, faith-focused mindset.

"Now faith is confidence in what we hope for and assurance about what we do not see."
Hebrews 11:1 NIV

Aligning Your Beliefs

The process of aligning your convictions with Christian values is a personal journey involving a deep understanding, wholehearted acceptance, and the daily application of the core teachings and principles of Christianity.

Whether you are a seasoned Christian looking to fortify your faith or someone venturing into the realm of Christianity for the first time, this section is designed to provide insights into the foundational elements of the Christian faith.

The single most important belief as a Christian is the understanding and genuine certainty in only ONE God.

Isaiah 45:5-6 says, *"I am the Lord, and there is no other; apart from me there is no God. I will strengthen you, though you have not acknowledged me, so that from the rising of the sun to the place of its setting people may know there is none besides me. I am the Lord, and there is no other."*

It is equally important, as Christians, to align with the belief that Jesus is the Son of God.

"As soon as Jesus was baptized, he went up out of the water. At that moment heaven was opened, and he saw the Spirit of God descending like a dove and alighting on him. And a voice from heaven said, 'This is my Son, whom I love; with him I am well pleased," Matthew 3:16-17 NASB.

And of course, the most quoted verse that Christianity stands upon, *"For God so loved the world, he gave his only begotten Son, that whosoever believes in him shall not perish but have everlasting life,"* John 3:16 KJV.

Another central aspect of Christian belief is the unwavering acknowledgment that the Bible serves as the cornerstone text of Christianity.

It is essential to dedicate time to reading and studying both the Old and New Testaments to gain a profound understanding of the teachings, stories, and values it encapsulates.

If the enormity of the Bible feels intimidating, consider starting with the Gospels, namely Matthew, Mark, Luke, and John, which offer a comprehensive account of the life of Jesus Christ.

Within these texts, focus your attention on the teachings of Jesus, particularly the Sermon on the Mount, outlined in Matthew 5-7. These teachings are a resounding call to embrace core Christian values, such as love, forgiveness, humility, and compassion, which are central to the Christian faith.

Colossians 3:16 NASB says, *"Let the word of Christ richly dwell within you, with all wisdom teaching and admonishing one another with psalms and hymns and spiritual songs, singing with thankfulness in your hearts to God."*

As Christians, faith often involves trusting in something beyond your immediate understanding or control. Life can present challenges that test your faith, especially concerning money, finances, and wealth.

Develop resilience by viewing these challenges as opportunities for growth and learning to rely on your faith to navigate them. Incorporate acts of kindness and service into your daily life. Reaching out to others with acts of kindness and embracing compassion is a powerful way to express your faith, as it allows you to become a living testament to Christ's work.

Through these actions, you embody and exemplify His guiding principles in your daily life.

Another fundamental aspect of faith is to nurture a mindset of gratitude for the many blessings and abundance that grace your life.

This is a point I consider significant and will explore it in greater depth later in this book. The ability to recognize and appreciate the goodness that surrounds you can significantly reinforce your faith and strengthen your trust in God.

Moreover, it is a worthy pursuit to seek inner peace and contentment. A faith-focused mindset often paves the way for tranquility and an enhanced capacity to find contentment in life's ups and downs.

Share your faith and experiences with others so that they may benefit from your personal journey. This can be a way to inspire and support others on their paths.

Remember that developing a faith-focused mindset is a personal and ongoing process. It will take time, and your journey may evolve over the years.

Be patient with yourself, allow your faith to grow organically as you align the connection with your beliefs and God.

Cultivating Trust in God

Cultivating trust in God is a central theme throughout the Bible. The Bible offers numerous verses, stories, and teachings that can inspire and guide you on your financial journey to trust in God.

Here are some key Bible verses and passages to remind you to cultivate your trust in God. Save these, either here in this book or in your Bible; you will return to many of these during your journey to prosperity.

> Proverbs 3:5-6 NIV: *"Trust in the Lord with all your heart and lean not on your own understanding; in all your ways submit to him, and he will make your paths straight."*

> Jeremiah 17:7-8 NIV: *"But blessed is the one who trusts in the Lord, whose confidence is in him. They will be like a tree planted by the water that sends out its roots by the stream. It does not fear when heat comes; its leaves are always green. It*

has no worries in a year of drought and never fails to bear fruit."

Psalms 37:3-5 NIV: *"Trust in the Lord and do good; dwell in the land and enjoy safe pasture. Take delight in the Lord, and he will give you the desires of your heart. Commit your way to the Lord; trust in him and he will do this."*

Psalms 62:8 NIV: *"Trust in him at all times, you people; pour out your hearts to him, for God is our refuge."*

Romans 15:13 NIV: *"May the God of hope fill you with all joy and peace as you trust in him, so that you may overflow with hope by the power of the Holy Spirit."*

Matthew 6:25-27 NIV: *"Therefore I tell you, do not worry about your life, what you will eat or drink; or about your body, what you will wear. Is not life more than food, and the body more than clothes? Look at the birds of the air; they do not sow or reap or store away in barns, and yet your heavenly Father feeds them. Are you not much more valuable than they?"*

In the realm of financial matters, these verses and passages from the Bible offer more than monetary advice; they provide a transformative guide for cultivating trust in God and fostering a positive, faith-filled mindset in the realm of wealth management.

Placing your trust in God is not only a spiritual principle but also a practical approach to any decision-making. By seeking refuge in Him and relying on His unwavering guidance and faithfulness, you establish a foundation for financial decisions rooted in divine wisdom.

The importance behind integrating trust in God into financial management lies in its potential to bring about a holistic transformation. Trusting in God with your finances can provide a sense of peace and assurance amid economic uncertainties, reminding you that there is a higher purpose guiding your financial journey.

Just as Abraham, Moses, and David trusted in God's plan for their lives, studying these important stories can inspire and provide practical insights into navigating challenges with unwavering trust and faith.

Ultimately, cultivating trust in God into your positive faith-focused mindset is not just a spiritual exercise but a strategic choice that aligns your financial decisions with timeless principles, fostering a faith-filled approach to wealth management.

Overcoming Negative Mindset

It is easy to begin your walk with God and Jesus Christ with excitement and a burning passion. However, as life progresses and challenges present themselves (especially financial challenges), you may encounter old mindsets, especially negative ones.

Overcoming a negative mindset biblically involves seeking guidance and wisdom from the Bible to transform your thoughts and attitudes.

The Bible is a rich source of teachings and principles that can guide you in cultivating a more positive and faith-filled mindset. When you disassociate yourself from negative things your life and your mindset changes drastically.

Romans 12:2 NIV says, *"Do not conform to the pattern of this world, but be transformed by the renewing of your mind."*

Meditate on this verse and commit to renewing your mind through the Word of God. It is a practice worth embracing to renew your faith continually.

Incorporate a regular practice of reading, praying, and meditating on uplifting passages from the Bible into your daily routine.

As Psalms 119:105 NIV beautifully puts it, *"Your word is a lamp for my feet, a light on my path."*

The Bible serves as a guiding light, steering your thoughts towards a more positive and hopeful direction. Pay attention to the words you speak, both about yourself and your circumstances.

Sometimes, it is necessary to verbalize encouragements as it can be a powerful method to counter any objections your mind might raise. A valuable exercise in this journey is to offer yourself kindness by speaking positively to your reflection in the mirror.

Engage in self-encouragement and nurturing self-talk. For instance, rather than dwelling on what you might dislike, choose to focus on something you genuinely appreciate about yourself.

I began this practice years ago to combat my own self-deprecating thoughts. I started with my eyes, admiring their unique color, and gradually expanded my affirmations to encompass my whole being.

Over time, these affirmative words transformed my self-perception, and I began to genuinely believe in my own beauty and worth.

This simple yet profound act can be a catalyst for a more positive and self-affirming mindset.

Remember the wisdom of Proverbs 18:21 NIV, which reminds us that *"the tongue has the power of life and death."*

Make the conscious choice to speak life and hope into your existence. There is an incredible power in speaking positive words to transform your perspective.

When you consciously embrace positivity in language and self-talk, you plant seeds of hope and resilience in your own mind. By replacing self-doubt, fear, and negativity with affirming you will gradually shift your mindset towards optimism.

In addition, free yourself from the burden of bitterness, anger, or lingering grudges. Letting go of these negative emotions can significantly contribute to your positive mindset and overall well-being.

Ephesians 4:31-32 NIV teaches, *"Get rid of all bitterness, rage, and anger, brawling and slander, along with every form of malice. Be kind and compassionate to one another, forgiving each other, just as in Christ God forgave you."*

One of the most powerful ways to break free from a negative mindset is through the simple act of forgiveness, both for others and for yourself. It is an act of liberation that can pave the way for a brighter, more faith-infused perspective.

I have found that sometimes, the toughest place to discover grace is within our own minds. So, make it a practice to extend grace and understanding to yourself and accept that, just like all of us, you are imperfect, but perfect in God's eyes.

Recognizing and acknowledging negative thoughts when they arise is another excellent practice.

Proverbs 4:23 NIV reminds us, *"Above all else, guard your heart, for everything you do flows from it."*

One of the phrases often said in life is, "The longest 18 inches of your life is between your head and your heart."

It is easy to fall into a negative mindset while the heart screams for you to be positive. Counter these negative thoughts with biblical truths.

For example, if you are feeling anxious, meditate on Philippians 4:6-7 NIV, which encourages you not to be worried about anything.

"Do not be anxious about anything, but in every situation, by prayer and petition, with thanksgiving, present your requests to God. And the peace of God, which transcends all understanding, will guard your hearts and your minds in Christ Jesus."

Seek God's help in transforming your thoughts. Pray for a renewed mind and the strength to overcome negativity.

James 1:5 NIV assures us, *"If any of you lacks wisdom, you should ask God, who gives generously to all without finding fault, and it will be given to you."*

Practice gratitude daily, as 1 Thessalonians 5:16-18 NIV advises, *"Rejoice always, pray continually, give thanks in all circumstances; for this is God's will for you in Christ Jesus."*

Gratitude can shift your focus from what is negative to what is positive. Gratitude in God will provide for generations.

Psalms 100:4-5 says, *"Enter His gates with thanksgiving and his courts with praise; give thanks to Him and praise His name. For the Lord is good and His love endures forever; His faithfulness continues through all generations."*

His faithfulness – His provision – continues through all generations.

Place your trust in God's sovereignty and His plan for your life, including prosperity.

Too many times, Christians allow hope and love, but refuse to allow prosperity from God out of belief it is not from Him.

Jeremiah 29:11 NIV reminds us, *"For I know the plans I have for you, declares the Lord, plans to prosper you and not to harm you, plans to give you hope and a future."*

It is important to keep in mind that overcoming a negative mindset is a process, one that might require time and dedicated effort.

During this transformative journey, place your trust in God's boundless grace and His guiding hand. Be patient with yourself as you labor to realign your thoughts and attitudes with His Word.

Chapter 3: Prayer and Manifestation

The first two chapters of this book have laid the foundation of fundamental Christian values, biblical teachings on Christian wealth, faith-focused mindset, and trust in God.

The power of prayer in manifesting abundance lies in the ability to cultivate a positive mindset, promote gratitude, and manifest intentions with God's help.

I believe it is important to start with the dictionary definition of manifest/manifestation because this is the part of prayer and meditation associated with not being inherently Christian.

In various contexts, manifestation can refer to the physical appearance of something, the demonstration of a quality or characteristic, or the realization of a goal or intention, among other meanings.

The term is used in various fields, including spirituality, psychology, and everyday language, to describe the evident expression of something previously concealed or abstract. Merriam-Webster defines manifestation as this:

Manifestation:
1:   *a: the act, process, or an instance of manifesting*
        b: something that manifests or is manifest.
        c: readily perceived by the senses and especially sense of sight.
        d: easily understood or recognized by the mind.
        e: a perceptible, outward, or visible expression

The concept of manifestation, as understood in modern self-help and personal development circles, may be found in Bible passages that contain principles and teachings such as faith, positive thinking, and the power of belief.

Jesus manifested loaves of bread and fish to feed thousands. This is one of the most prolific examples of manifestation.

Prayer in a Christian context is a conversation you have with God internally and sometimes spoken. Now, look at the definition of prayer in the Merriam-Webster dictionary.

Prayer:
1: an address (such as a petition) to God or a god in word or thought
        a: a set order of words used in praying.
        b: an earnest request or wish.
        c: act or practice of praying to God or a god kneeling in prayer[1]

Some people only pray set prayers such as the Lord's Prayer as Jesus gave in the Sermon on the Mount.

"Pray, then, in this way: 'Our Father who is in heaven, Hallowed be Your name. Your kingdom come. Your will be done, On earth as it is in heaven. Give us this day our daily bread. And forgive us our debts, as we also have forgiven our debtors. And do not lead us into temptation, but deliver us from evil. [For Yours is the kingdom and the power and the glory forever. Amen.']"

---

[1] Merriam-Webster Online, 2023

Others pray by conversing with God internally while doing something like driving down the road, listening to music, cleaning the house, etc.

The Law of Attraction and Manifestation

Let us begin with the principles within the Law of Attraction since in modern day it is the most notable concept attached to the word *"manifestation."*

The Law of Attraction is a concept popularized in modern self-help and personal development literature, most of which came about in the 1800s and then reiterated in the late 1950s to early 2000s.

Incidentally, the "New Thought Movement" has origins in the teachings of Plato and Phineas Parkhurst Quimby – who believed he had rediscovered the healing methods of Jesus.

The 1917 St. Louis Congress (Missouri) adopted the "Declaration of Principles," and modified them in 1919 and again in 2000. The principles included variations of the Law of Attraction. Which is often described in principle that 'like attracts like,' meaning that the energy and thoughts you put into the universe will return similar energy and circumstances to you.

It suggests that positive thoughts and beliefs can attract positive outcomes, while negative thoughts and ideas can attract adverse outcomes.

Key components of the Law of Attraction include positive thinking, visualization, affirmations, gratitude, and action.

Advocates of the Law of Attraction stress the importance of maintaining a positive mindset. They believe cultivating positive thoughts and emotions is crucial for attracting positive experiences and outcomes.

Visualization is a technique that involves imagining yourself already in possession of the desired result. Visualizing your goals strengthens your belief in them and attracts them into your reality.

Affirmations are positive statements or phrases that individuals repeat to themselves regularly. These affirmations reinforce beliefs in one's ability to achieve one's goals and attract what one desires.

The Law of Attraction is a subjective belief system and is not universally accepted or scientifically proven. Some people find it to be a helpful tool for personal development, positive mindset, and goal setting, while others approach it with skepticism.

The Law of Attraction is often linked to specific interpretations of quantum physics theories, but it is important to clarify that the connection is not recognized within the scientific community.

The idea that consciousness or observation can affect physical reality is sometimes cited as the main parallel between Quantum Physics and the Law of Attraction. Particles like atoms and electrons can exist in multiple states simultaneously, a concept known as superposition.

They can also be mysteriously connected over large distances, a phenomenon called entanglement. What is even more mind-boggling is that when you try to observe these particles, our measurements can affect their behavior, leading to the famous Heisenberg Uncertainty Principle.

Proponents of the Law of Attraction argue that just as the act of observation in quantum physics can influence the outcome, so too can the power of focused thought affect one's life circumstances.

Many physicists and scientists reject the idea that quantum principles and mainstream science can be applied directly to personal development or metaphysical beliefs like the Law of Attraction.

This association is a matter of personal belief and interpretation; it is not a scientifically established connection and remains a debate topic within the scientific and self-help communities.

Now that you have a simplified understanding of the Law of Attraction regarding Physics, specifically Quantum Physics, and that it is not a scientifically based law. I want to help you understand how the Law of Attraction relates to manifestation.

Earlier, I defined manifestation within the context of the English language as "an act, process, or instance manifesting – readily perceived by the senses and especially by the sense of sight; Easily understood or recognized by the mind."

Therefore, for comparative purposes, I will define it in the context of the Law of Attraction.

"There are many different definitions of the word manifestation, but the simplest would be that it is 'something that is put into your physical reality through thought, feelings, and beliefs. This means that whatever you focus on is what you are bringing into your reality. You may focus and manifest through meditation, visualization, or just via your conscious or subconscious." (Lawofattraction.com, 2023)

Doesn't that sound a lot like prayer to you?

I want to repeat one part: "Whatever you focus on is what you are bringing into your reality."

Again, the Bible says in Matthew 21:22 NIV: *"If you believe, you will receive whatever you ask for in prayer."* and Mark 11:24 NIV: *"Therefore I tell you, whatever you ask for in prayer, believe that you have received it, and it will be yours."*

These are the absolute basic fundamentals of the Law of Attraction and Manifestation. You manifest your visions, feelings, and beliefs through prayer and through meditation with God. This is such an "AH HA" moment for all Christians.

You absolutely can pray, seek, and receive, making manifest in your life with God.

Now, digging deeper into manifestation, the Bible uses the word manifest in various contexts over eleven times.

In the King James Version, it is used precisely eleven times; in the New American Standard Version, it appears thirteen times; and in the New International Version, it is used seventeen times.

Jesus manifested to the disciples, in other words he appeared visible to them after death:

"After these things Jesus manifested Himself again to the disciples at the Sea of Tiberias" John 21:1 NASB, which in essence is the literal definition of a manifest.

Jesus manifested himself in multiple places to Mary Magdelene (Mark 16:9), the disciples (Luke 24:15-31), and a crowd of five hundred after the resurrection (1 Corinthians 15:6).

Remember, manifesting is something that is not visible will appear visible.

In the second chapter of the Gospel of John, Jesus demonstrated a different form of manifestation.

This account narrates a miracle that took place at a wedding in Cana of Galilee, showcasing a unique way in which Jesus revealed his divine power.

The wedding was in full swing when the hosts ran out of wine, which could have caused embarrassment and concern. Mary, the mother of Jesus, who knew of her son's extraordinary abilities, turned to him for help.

Jesus instructed the servants to fill six stone jars with water, which he then turned into the finest wine, saving the day and ensuring the celebrations continued with even greater joy.

This story is a symbol of manifestation, abundance, and the blessings that Jesus brings into our lives.

John 2:11 NASB says, *"This beginning of His signs Jesus did in Cana of Galilee, and manifested His glory, and His disciples believed in Him."*

Jesus manifested water into wine while simultaneously manifesting Himself as the Son of God in the eyes of his disciples. The NIV version of this verse uses the word "revealed' in place of manifested.

Luke 8:17 KJV, Jesus speaks of manifestation as *"For nothing is secret, that shall not be made manifest; neither anything hid, that shall not be known or come abroad."*

The NIV translation uses the word "disclosed," and the NASB uses the word "evident" for this same verse.

As you read the Bible for yourself, note the interchangeability of the word "manifest" with the words "revealed, evident, and disclosed," throughout the Bible.

Manifestation versus Prayer

"If you believe, you will receive whatever you ask for in prayer."
Matthew 21:22 NIV

Matthew 21:22 encapsulates a fundamental biblical principle that beautifully links the power of prayer with the concept of manifesting one's faith and desires.

Mark 11:24 NIV states: *"Therefore I tell you, whatever you ask for in prayer, believe that you have received it, and it will be yours."*

This verse emphasizes the importance of faith and desires when praying for something, again a fundamental aspect of manifestation.

You will find that these verses underscore the significance of prayer and meditation to connect with God, and receiving abundantly what you ask for in prayer.

As you embark on your personal manifestation journey, you may uncover profound inspiration within specific verses, much like I have. So, how do you connect prayer with manifesting abundance? The bible gives us several references such as:

Philippians 4:13 NIV: "I can do all this through him who gives me strength."

This verse can be interpreted as a declaration of empowerment and belief in one's ability to achieve goals with the help of God.

Proverbs 23:7 KJV: "For as he thinketh in his heart, so is he."
This verse highlights that one's thoughts and beliefs significantly impact one's reality, which aligns with the principle of positive thinking and manifestation.

James 1:5-6 NIV: "If any of you lacks wisdom, you should ask God, who gives generously to all without finding fault, and it will be given to you. But when you ask, you must believe and not doubt, because the one who doubts is like a wave of the sea, blown and tossed by the wind."

If there is one message in this book that I hope truly resonates with you, it is this particular verse. It underlines the unwavering importance of belief and trust when we seek guidance and blessings through prayer. It is worth noting that interpretations of these passages can differ, and not all Christians or scholars may immediately connect these verses with the modern concept of manifestation.

In the context of personal development, manifestation often revolves around material desires and goals, while these Bible passages primarily address faith, prayer, and spiritual matters.

Nonetheless, my goal is to illustrate how the principles behind the "New Thought Movement" and "Law of Attraction" manifestation techniques are rooted in biblical principles—principles that are inherently Christian beliefs. It is about recognizing the spiritual foundation that underlies these concepts.

Earlier, I touched on gratitude in the context of overcoming negative thoughts, yet expressing gratitude for what you already have is also considered an essential part of Manifestation.

Gratitude, as it is taught within the Law of Attraction manifestation technique, is believed to raise your vibrational frequency, and attract more positive experiences into your life. While the Law of Attraction emphasizes the power of thoughts and beliefs, it does not negate the need for action.

Advocates suggest that positive thinking and belief should accompany inspired action toward your goals. Proponents of the Law of Attraction often cite some Bible verses because they contain principles related to thoughts, beliefs, and the power of faith. For example, let us look at one of the verses above but stated in a way that aligns with aspects of the Law of Attraction.

Proverbs 23:7 KJV: "For as he thinketh in his heart, so is he." This verse emphasizes the influence of one's thoughts and beliefs on one's life, which is a core idea in the Law of Attraction.
I am going to expand with a few other verses.

Mark 11:24 NIV: "Therefore I tell you, whatever you ask for in prayer, believe that you have received it, and it will be yours." I already used this as it highlights the importance of faith and belief in the context of prayer and desires. However, it also aligns with the Law of Attraction's emphasis on belief and visualization.

Matthew 21:22 NIV: "If you believe, you will receive whatever you ask for in prayer."

This verse underscores the significance of belief and faith when seeking blessings through prayer, another core principle of the Law of Attraction.

Philippians 4:8 NIV: "Finally, brothers and sisters, whatever is true, whatever is noble, whatever is right, whatever is pure, whatever is lovely, whatever is admirable—if anything is excellent or praiseworthy—think about such things."

This verse encourages positive and uplifting thoughts, central to the Law of Attraction's focus on maintaining a positive mindset.

It is important to note that these Bible verses were not originally written with the Law of Attraction manifestation in mind – the concept did not exist when the Bible was written.

The 'Law of Attraction' and any other secret to success you may have read about are not new concepts. The verses in this section primarily address faith, prayer, meditation, overcoming limiting beliefs, and the power of thoughts within a spiritual context.

Interpretations of these verses in relation to the Law of Attraction can vary widely, and not all Christians or scholars would necessarily make such connections.

The point here is that the intentions behind the new thought movements and manifestations are variations from the verses in the Bible that have existed long before anyone had a 'new thought.'

Individuals can find inspiration in these verses and may incorporate principles of faith, belief, and positive thinking into their personal development journey.

However, I reiterate that it is crucial to approach these verses with respect for their original context and intended meaning within the Christian faith.

The Power of Prayer in Attracting Abundance

In your own journey of exploration, you may have noticed that Law of Attraction manifestation and Christian prayer are distinct yet intriguingly similar concepts.

Those who practice and experience the Law of Attraction manifesting, focus on self-realized unique goals and desires, envisioning a path to their fulfillment. In contrast, during moments of prayer you engage in heartfelt conversations with God, seeking divine guidance, blessings, and help not only for yourself but for others as well.

A positive mindset is essential in both practices. The Law of Attraction manifestation is about maintaining an optimistic outlook, believing that your thoughts and actions hold the power to shape your reality.

In prayer, it is a deep faith in God's influence on your reality and a resolute belief in His providence and grace. Manifesting may fill you with temporary excitement and motivation as you vividly picture your goals coming to fruition.

Yet in prayer, you will find yourself enveloped in feelings of comfort, peace, and a profound connection with God – a longer, sustainable goal and desire. Both practices can contribute to personal growth and self-improvement, but the Bible warns you to not be deceived by hollow practices like the Law of Attraction. "

See to it that no one takes you captive through hollow and deceptive philosophy, which depends on human tradition and the elemental spiritual forces of this world rather than on Christ," Colossians 2:8 NIV.

Now, let us shift the focus away from the Law of Attraction and focus solely on praying and manifesting in the Christian context. When you pray for abundance, you focus your thoughts and energy on your desires, which can help us clarify our goals and aspirations.

However, one significant insight here is that when you pray for your desires and clarify your goals – especially concerning financial abundance – you must do so from a place of expanding the Kingdom of God.

It is essential to anchor your desires in God rather than letting them be driven solely by selfish, ego-driven motives.

James 4:3 NIV warns, *"When you ask, you do not receive, because you ask with wrong motives, that you may spend what you get on your pleasures."*

When your requests and prayers align with God's purpose, He will graciously honor them. In this divine exchange, you not only benefit from the abundance but also contribute to the growth and unity of the community dedicated to building the Kingdom of God.

Prayer will provide hope and faith, reducing stress and anxiety associated with financial worries.

Philippians 4:6-7 NIV states: *"Do not be anxious about anything but in every situation, by prayer and petition, with thanksgiving, present your requests to God. And the peace of God, which transcends all understanding, will guard your hearts and your minds in Christ Jesus."*

By consistently expressing gratitude for the blessings that you already have and asking for guidance and abundance, you align yourself with God's potential to provide opportunities and resources that can lead to greater prosperity.

"Rejoice always; pray without ceasing; in everything give thanks; for this is God's will for you in Christ Jesus," 1 Thessalonians 5:16-18 NASB.

Prayer alone will not guarantee instant wealth; it can be a powerful tool for creating a mindset conducive to abundance and taking inspired action toward our goals.

Ecclesiastes 5:19 NASB says, *"Furthermore, as for every man to whom God has given riches and wealth, He has also empowered him to eat from them and to receive his reward and rejoice in his labor; this is the gift from God."*

The beautiful reminder in Ecclesiastes 5:19 serves to acknowledge God's role in the acquisition of wealth and to use prayer for guidance on how to use that wealth wisely.

Your prayer becomes the channel for you to align your intentions with God's higher purpose, fostering a mindset that goes beyond mere accumulation and spending.

Ultimately, the power of prayer will connect you personally to God and provide you with a sense of peace, purpose, and resilience on your journey toward greater abundance.

Trusting God's Timing

"Blessed is the one who trusts in the Lord, whose confidence is in him." Jeremiah 17:7 NIV

Trusting God's timing is a profound lesson in patience, faith, and surrender.

Psalms 27:14 NIV reminds all to *"Wait for the Lord; be strong and take heart and wait for the Lord."*

It means recognizing that there is a divine plan at work in our lives, even when circumstances seem uncertain or challenging. Just as a seed must wait for the right season to bloom, you, too, must have faith that God's timing is perfect.

"When I am afraid, I put my trust in you. In God, whose word I praise – in God I trust and am not afraid," Psalms 56:3-4 NIV.

This trust allows us to release the anxiety of trying to control everything and, instead, embrace the unfolding of our lives with grace and patience. It means understanding that delays and setbacks can be opportunities for growth and learning, leading you to a better outcome than you could have imagined.

"There is a time for everything and a season for every activity under the heavens," Ecclesiastes 3:1 NIV.

Trusting in God's perfect timing is like letting go and saying, "God, I trust Your wisdom even when I cannot see the whole picture. Your plans for my life are always for my best."

It reminds me of Isaiah 40:31 NIV from the Bible, where it says, *"But those who hope in the Lord will renew their strength. They will soar on wings like eagles; they will run and not grow weary, they will walk and not be faint."*

You see, it is about having faith that no matter what season of life you are in, whether you are soaring high like an eagle or trudging through a tough period, there is a purpose behind it all.

God's timing is always spot on, even when it does not align with our own plans. So, let us remember to trust in His perfect timing, knowing that He's working behind the scenes for our ultimate good, and that we can find renewed strength and hope in Him.

Effectively Praying to Manifest Financial Blessings

Effective prayer strategies for abundance involve a combination of biblical principles, a positive mindset, and specific techniques. Using gratitude and coming from a place of gratefulness is one of the most effective ways to pray for all things, not just for abundance.

Start your prayers with gratitude. Express thanks for the blessings and abundance you already have in your life. Cultivating an attitude of gratitude sets a positive tone for your prayers.

"Whatever you do in word or deed, do all in the name of Lord Jesus, giving thanks through Him to God the Father." Colossians 3:17 NASB

"But thanks be to God, who always leads us in triumph in Christ, and manifests through us the sweet aroma of the knowledge of Him in every place." 2 Corinthians 2:14 NASB

When you are praying for financial abundance, be extremely specific. Clearly define what abundance means to you and what you are asking for. Do not just ask God to give you lots of money. That is not an honorable request, as it is self-serving.

Instead, ask God to bless you with an abundance of money in your finances so you may give heartily to the community and your church to grow the Kingdom of God.

You can be more specific about how much but be cautious not to pray for it by a specific date or manner.

For example: Do not pray, "Let me win the lottery jackpot this Saturday." That is not an effective prayer.

Instead, pray and ask God to provide you with a financial abundance over $2.5 million so you may give to the church that needs a new building.

You are being specific for a purpose that fulfills a need in the community, centered on God, not yourself. Will you personally gain financially from this type of prayer – sure. But the goal is not your personal financial wealth; it is so that you may provide for the church and build in the community.

Do not limit God to just one avenue of financial blessings, like the lottery, but be open to receiving from any source of abundance. You just never know who or what God is using to bless you and answer your prayers.

There is a powerful story of a missionary in Uganda, who possessed an unwavering faith in the power of manifestation and prayer.

His journey was an extraordinary testament to the belief that God's benevolence would provide for his every need. With a humble backpack slung over his shoulders and just a meager sum of money, he embarked on a mission that would change his life forever.

Upon reaching a small town in Uganda, he found shelter in the kindness of its people. However, they expected compensation for their hospitality, either in money or food, as he was a stranger from another country and not from their small village.

Slowly, his funds dwindled, but he refused to despair, for his faith in God's divine timing and provision remained unshaken.

As the missionary's journey neared its end, he found himself in a predicament.

His expenses had exceeded his expectations, leaving him with inadequate funds to secure a plane ticket for his journey home.

Additionally, the looming expiration of his visa only added to his mounting worries. Each day, he fervently prayed and visualized the money required for his plane ticket back home. Gratitude filled his heart as he trusted in God's ability to provide.

As the date for purchasing the ticket drew nearer, the expected miracle had yet to occur. For the first time, doubt began to creep into the missionary's mind, and he questioned why God seemed to be delaying his much-needed assistance.

One evening, as he confided his worries to a fellow missionary, a generous offer of a loan was extended. Yet, the missionary declined, convinced that he would receive the money from God in due time.

This was one of the few times the missionary had to set a deadline, not as a demand but out of sheer necessity. A few days later, while lying in the modest room he had been provided with, a profound thought filled his mind as if a divine message had been delivered. "I gave you the money, but you refused it," resounded in his thoughts.

Startled, he sat up, staring at the ceiling in disbelief. He had always expected God to provide in a certain way, but it had not occurred to him that God might choose to work through his friend's generosity.

A sense of relief washed over him, but guilt accompanied it. The answer to his prayers had been right in front of him, but he had dismissed it because it did not align with his preconceived idea for how God would provide.

He eventually accepted the money from his friend, enabling him to return to his home country.

The missionary learned a profound lesson: God always answers, but His provision does not always conform to our expectations. His blessings may come in unexpected ways, through unanticipated channels, or in forms we do not immediately recognize.

To truly experience God's promise and provision, you must have unshakable faith, trust in His timing, and exercise patience. Instead of limiting God to your expectations, you should allow His divine plan to unfold, fulfilling your needs and desires in the most unexpected and miraculous ways.

1 John 5:14-15 NIV: "This is the confidence we have in approaching God: that if we ask anything according to His will, He hears us. And if we know that he hears us – whatever we ask – we know that we have what we asked of Him."

Jeremiah 29:11 NIV: "For I know the plans I have for you," declares the Lord, "plans to prosper you and not to harm you, plans to give you hope and a future."

Approach your prayers with unwavering faith and believe that your request is possible. Do not question God's provision, or the way in which He provides, the Bible already asks the questions for you.

Matthew 7:11 NIV: "If you, then, though you are evil, know how to give good gifts to your children, how much more will your Father in heaven give good gifts to those who ask Him!"

Romans 8:32 NIV, "He who did not spare His own Son, but gave Him up for us all – how will He not also, along with Him, graciously give us all things?"

Another effective technique to manifest with God is to use visualization while praying; visualize yourself already possessing the abundance you seek.

Imagine the details and feelings associated with achieving your goals. Visualization can help reinforce your beliefs and desires. Choose a Bible verse that resonates with your current prayer or intention.

Close your eyes to block out all distractions and help you focus on your prayers and visions. Meditate on the Bible verses you have chosen and visualize the scene, the verse coming to life, or the message that the verse conveys.

Use your imagination to engage your senses.

For example, if you were to use the verse Psalm 65:11 NIV, *"You crown the year with your bounty and your carts overflow with abundance,"* you might truly visualize money or checks overflowing from a cart, a wagon, or a tote while you push it toward the church.

Allow yourself to smile and feel the emotions associated with the verse. If you choose a verse on gratitude, feel the warmth of thankfulness in your heart.

As you visualize and feel, let your heart guide your prayer. Speak to God in your own words, expressing your thoughts, feelings, and desires in connection with the verse(s).

Sometimes, during this type of visualization, you may receive clarity about your prayers or the verse's meaning. Be open to these insights and revelations.

It is highly important that once you have lifted your prayers to God, let go of attachment to the outcomes. Trust that God will provide in His own time and way. Surrendering control can alleviate anxiety and impatience.

Consider including requests for opportunities to help others to make a positive impact in your prayers. Prayers should be accompanied by efforts and actions that align with your desires, do not just pray then do nothing.

Abundance often comes because of your efforts that help God provide an avenue of abundance.

Pray within a Bible study group, from a prayer list, or seek support from like-minded individuals who share your beliefs and abundance goals. Group prayers and support can amplify the effectiveness of your intentions. *"For where two or three have gathered together in My name, I am there in their midst,"* Matthew 18:20 NASB.

Maintain a prayer journal to record your prayers, manifestations, and any signs or guidance you receive. Reflecting on your journey can help you stay motivated and track your progress.

Effective prayer strategies for abundance should encompass all aspects of a grateful heart, a specific God-centered goal, and true trust and belief in God and His plan to fulfill our prayers.

"Delight yourself in the Lord, And He will give you the desires of your heart." Psalms 37:4.

Manifestation P.R.A.Y.E.R.™ method

A new effective technique that you can use is the Manifestation P.R.A.Y.E.R.™ method.

The P.R.A.Y.E.R.™ method is a simplified way to structure a manifestation prayer with God. It is best to do this alone in a quiet space without distractions.

Once you master this technique, you can use it in anything you want to manifest through God. Let us break down the method.

P – Practice Mindfulness and Gratitude

- Start from a place of thankfulness for all you already have. Find a grateful heart and feel it deeply. Truly practice appreciation for God and His works, which paves the way for greater financial abundance. *Rejoice always; pray without ceasing; in everything give thanks; for this is God's will for you in Christ Jesus.* 1 Thessalonians 5:16-18 NASB.
- Come from a place of positivity. (i.e., Money flows to me abundantly from God for His glory; I am worthy of God's grace and abundance)

- Overcome any negative beliefs you may encounter. Use scripture as your foundation! (i.e., Instead of I can't do this – think *I can do all things through Christ which strengthens me – Philippians 4:13 KJV*)

R – Reflect on Your True Intentions

- Reflect on your true intentions, calling from your heart your real "Why?"
- Be sure to reflect with scripture and Bible study to ensure your desires/intentions are set for the glory of God.
- If you find that your true intention is self-serving and not for God's purpose for your life, ask God to show you your path – turn your selfishness into light. *"You, Lord, are my lamp; the Lord turns my darkness into light,"* 2 Samuel 22:29 NIV.
- Regularly review and adjust your desires and intentions, repeating as necessary until you are aligned in Christ.

A – Align in Christ, and Accept any Insights

- Listen to your intuition, your gut, and your feelings. God speaks to you through these. If you are reflecting on your intentions and desires, and you hear a 'still small voice' speaking to you, listen to it. *"How precious also are Your thoughts to me, O God! How vast is the sum of them!"* Psalms 139:17 NASB.
- Set Christ-inspired goals. Use the SMART goal-setting method[2] keeping God the center focus of your goals. Rather than making a vague prayer for financial blessings, you can be specific in our requests. Here is an example: you might pray for $15,000 to achieve financial security in your home life, viewing it as a testimony to the gifts bestowed by God. With the intention of giving $1,500 to the church building fund in

---

[2] See Chapter 4 for the SMART goal setting method.

the next three to six months, your goal becomes inherently God-centered and specific.

- Visualize your intentions and desires coming true with God receiving all the glory! If you desire to increase your monthly pay to give more, envision the check you write to the charity or church. Imagine your hand giving the check over and feel the cheerful feelings in the satisfaction of being able to give. *"The point is this: whoever sows sparingly will also reap sparingly, and whoever sows bountifully will also reap bountifully. Each one must give as he has decided in his heart, not reluctantly or under compulsion, **for God loves a cheerful giver,**"* 2 Corinthians 9:6-7 NIV. Feel the cheerfulness in your heart as you envision giving. Remember, it helps to have scripture as a reference to feel and visualize.

Y – YAHWEH – Believe in God and Trust in His Timing

- Believing in God and expressing genuine gratitude are key. You can trust His divine power to bring your desires to reality. *Luke 18:27 "What is impossible with man is possible with God."*
- Meditate deeply with God and let His presence guide you towards abundance. *Make me understand the way of Your precepts, So I will meditate on Your wonders,"* Psalms 119:27 NASB.
- Trust God completely and have faith that HIS timing is always perfect. Remembering that patience is one of the fruits of the spirit. Reflect and humble yourself to God's timing.

E – Effective Action

- Take your plan of action to God and ask for His guidance on these plans. Inspired actions include education, financial planning, debt reduction, etc. Use scripture references to help guide you. *"All Scripture is inspired by God and profitable for teaching, for reproof, for correction, for training in righteousness; so that the man of God may be adequate, equipped for every good work,"* 2 Timothy 3:16-17 NASB.

- Effective action means following the steps of your plan, knowing God has established your steps. *"The mind of man plans his way, But the Lord directs his steps,"* Proverbs16:9 NASB.
- Praying alone is not enough; it is essential to follow it with purposeful action. *"The way of the lazy is as a hedge of thorns, But the path of the upright is a highway,"* Proverbs 15:19 NASB. Like the story of the man who wanted to win the lottery, he prayed and prayed every day for it. After long praying, God finally answered him and said, "I can't answer your prayer if you do not buy a ticket." Give it to God but do your part; take effective action after your Manifestation P.R.A.Y.E.R.

R – Render to God

- Render it over to God, let go of the outcome or the way it will happen, and do not box God into an exact date or way to answer your prayer - like an ultimatum. Allow God to fulfill your manifestation in any way He deems for it to occur. You never know how, who or what God is using to fulfill your request.
- Give glory, praise, and honor to God as if prayers are already fulfilled. Believe your prayer has been answered. *Mark 11:24 NIV: "Therefore I tell you, whatever you ask for in prayer, believe that you have received it, and it will be yours."*
- End your Manifestation prayer in a way that confirms your belief and gratitude. (i.e., "I pray this trusting and believing in You." "In Jesus' name, I pray…")

"Whatever you ask in My name, this I will do, that the Father may be glorified in the Son." John 14:13 NASB

Sample Prayer:

Heavenly Father,

I approach you with a heart filled with gratitude and positive intent. I take a moment to reflect on my true intentions, ensuring they align with your divine purpose. I believe that you will provide for my needs as I embark on this journey. With unwavering faith, I commit to taking effective action, knowing that you guide my steps. I understand that my efforts are a form of rendering unto you, my dedication to your will. May my desires be in harmony with your plan for me, and may your blessings flow abundantly. In the name of Christ, I offer this prayer, trusting that you will lead me on the path to fulfillment.

Amen.

Chapter 4: Financial Goal Setting Through Faith

In this transformative chapter, you will explore the profound intersection of faith and financial goal setting, rooted in the belief that seeking God's guidance is the cornerstone of purposeful goal setting, you will embark on a journey to honor His will through the integration of faith-inspired financial objectives.

By establishing priorities grounded in faith, you not only chart a course for your financial well-being but also align yourself with the ultimate success envisioned by God.

Central to this process is the pivotal role of trust—trusting in God's guidance and surrendering control to His wisdom. This chapter unfolds a faith-fueled approach to financial planning, offering practical steps that seamlessly weave trust in God's guidance into our everyday financial decisions.

Through compelling examples, biblical references, and real-life testimonials, this will illuminate the path for you to set God-inspired financial goals, embrace unwavering trust in divine guidance, and infuse faith into every facet of your financial planning.

God-Inspired Financial Goals

The Bible does not explicitly mention "goal setting" in modern terms, but it does contain verses and teachings that can be interpreted as guidance for setting and pursuing goals.

Proverbs 16:3 NIV says, *"Commit to the Lord whatever you do, and He will establish your plans,"* and *"Whoever gives heed to instruction prospers, and blessed is the one who trusts in the Lord,"* Proverbs 16:20 NIV.

These verses suggest the importance of seeking divine guidance when setting plans and pursuing goals.

Proverbs 21:5 NIV says, *"The plans of the diligent lead to profit as surely as haste leads to poverty."*

This emphasizes the value of careful planning and diligence.

"May he give you the desire of your heart and make all your plans succeed," Psalms 20:4 NIV.

This verse highlights seeking God's guidance and aligning one's desires with His will. While the Bible may not provide a step-by-step guide to modern goal setting, these verses suggest principles of seeking God's guidance, being diligent, and pursuing goals with a higher purpose.

Many Christians incorporate these principles into their approach to setting and pursuing personal goals.

In the Neurolinguistic Practitioner (NLP) world, there are two types of goal setting that are highly recommended. For the purpose of this book, I will use the well-formed outcome SMART method for setting goals while incorporating God into our methodology.

The SMART method, created by George T. Duran, stands for Specific and Simple, Measurable and Meaningful to God, Achievable, Realistic and Responsible/Ecological, and Times and Toward.[3]

---

[3] Found in the NLP Guidebook by Auspicium Limited.

S - Specific and Simple: Well-defined, Clear to anyone involved, especially between you and God, for you to state in your prayers and meditations.

M- Measurable and Meaningful to God: Knowing if the goal is obtainable and when it has been or will be achieved. Be careful here not to box God into a deadline.

A – Achievable: Agreement between you and God on what the goals should be – presented as a need now, in all areas of your life or just one (for our example, you will use the financial area, and is it achievable.)

R – Realistic and Responsible/Ecological: Within the availability of resources, knowledge, and time. You would not set a goal to go to the planet Pluto as it is not possible or realistic, nor has the know-how been discovered (at the time of this book being written, anyway).

T – Times and Toward: Enough time to achieve the goal, but not too much time, which can affect the outcome and performance.

Let's put it into a practical example:

S: I will start a new business selling products that honor God using recycled materials that better our planet and spread the message of love for God and Jesus Christ. I will use 1 Thessalonians 4:11 as my verse to meditate on.

M: I will spend at least two hours a day marketing my business and two hours a day searching for recycled materials to make the products. The rest of the day would be designing graphics.

A: I know other companies have been successful selling recycled material products, so I know it is attainable. I have the ability to design prints for shirts and plastics that incorporate God and Jesus on them. I am also great at designing websites.

R: I know there is a vendor that uses recycled material shirts and plastics. I know I can get a bulk rate, and I can use the savings on the bulk product toward other expenses like website hosting. I will use ten percent of all sales toward my church's building fund.

T: I will have the business up and running, with the product ready to sell, within 90 days.

Based on this example the SMART goal to pray on: I will start a new ecologically friendly business within 90 days selling products that honor God while giving generously to my church.

Now, let's use this in a financial planning example:

S: I will have at least $15,000 in savings in 6 months, with the added goal to donate $1,500 of it to the local Christian women's shelter. I will pray using 1 Timothy 6:17-19.

M: I will transfer $575 from my checking account each week by automatic draft, so I do not forget, into my savings account. I will be able to view the account each week as the deposits are made to watch the progress.

A: I have $1000 in excess income each pay period, so I am going to curb my spending habits for the next six months and pray for perseverance to not spend the money in the savings account.

R: I want to give to the local Christian women's shelter so they can continue to witness to women and children, as well as clothe and feed them.

T: Tomorrow, I will put the automatic transfer protocols into my bank account app, setting up the transfer of money each week. I will not touch the savings account for 6 months. At the end of six months, I will write a check to the Christian Women's Shelter for $ 1,500 – 10% of my savings.

Based on this example the SMART goal to pray on: I will save $15,000 in 6 months by transferring $575 a week from my checking into my savings account while curbing my senseless spending, honoring God by giving 10% to the women's shelter at the end of the six months.

Below is a sample list of Christian Financial Goals to consider:

1. Tithing and Giving: Committing a portion of income, typically 10% (the tithe), to support one's local church and charitable causes. The topic of tithing is a very personal one, and because of that, this book will not get into the specifics of it. Just know that it is a common financial goal of Christians to be able to give to their church. Acts 20:35 NIV says, *"In everything I did, I showed you that by this kind of hard work we must help the weak, remembering the words the Lord himself said: 'it is more blessed to give than to receive.'"*

2. Debt Reduction: Striving to reduce or eliminate personal debt, following the teaching in Romans 13:8 NIV, *"Let no debt remain outstanding."* Proverbs 22:7 NIV advises, *"The rich rule over the poor, and the borrower is slave to the lender."* The Bible encourages prudent financial management and warns against excessive debt.

3. Saving and Emergency Fund: Building a savings account and emergency fund to ensure financial stability and provide for unexpected expenses, as advised in 1 Corinthians 16:2 NIV. *"On the first day of every week, each one of you should set aside a sum of money in keeping with your income, saving it up, so that when I come no collections will have to be made."*

4. Wise Stewardship: Managing finances responsibly and wisely, recognizing that all resources belong to God and should be used for His purposes. *"Whatever you do, work at it with all your heart, working for the Lord, not for human masters, since you know that you will receive an inheritance for the Lord as a reward. It is the Lord Christ you are serving,"* Colossians 3:23-24 NIV.

5. Retirement Planning: Preparing for retirement to ensure financial security in later years and not becoming a financial burden on others, in accordance with 1 Timothy 5:8 NASB. *"But if anyone does not provide for his own, and especially for those of his household, he has denied the faith and is worse than an unbeliever."*

6. Education and Skill Development: Investing in education and skill development to enhance one's ability to provide for oneself and one's family. *"How much better it is to get wisdom than gold! And to get understanding is to be chosen above silver,"* Proverbs 16:16 NASB.

7. Generosity: Setting goals for charitable giving and helping those in need, in alignment with Jesus' teachings in Matthew 25:35-36 and 40, NASB : *"For I was hungry, and you gave Me something to eat; I was thirsty, and you gave Me something to drink; I was a stranger, and you invited Me in; naked, and you clothed Me; I was sick, and you visited Me; I was in prison, and you came to Me."* And *"The King will answer and say to them, 'Truly I say to you, to the extent that you did it to one of these brothers of Mine, even the least of them, you did it to Me.'"*

8. Contentment: Cultivating contentment and avoiding materialism by focusing on the essentials of life, as emphasized in 1 Timothy 6:6-8 NIV. *"But godliness with contentment is great gain. For we brought nothing into the world, and we can take nothing out of it. But if we have food and clothing, we will be content with that."*

9. Financial Accountability: Holding oneself accountable for financial decisions and seeking counsel or guidance when needed, following the wisdom of Proverbs 15:22 NIV. *"Plans fail for lack of counsel, but with many advisers they succeed."*

10. Estate Planning: Preparing a will and estate plan to ensure that one's assets are distributed in accordance with one's wishes and values, as seen in Proverbs 13:22 NIV. *"A good person leaves an inheritance for their children's children, but a sinner's wealth is stored up for the righteous."*

It is necessary to point out that Christian financial goals may vary from person to person, depending on individual circumstances and values.

Setting these goals requires regular prayer, reflection, and seeking guidance from Christian financial advisors or mentors who can provide biblical wisdom and financial expertise.

The aim of Christian financial goals is to use money and resources in a way that honors God and contributes to one's spiritual growth and the well-being of others.

Trusting God's Guidance in Goal Setting

"Commit your way to the Lord; trust also in Him, and He will do it." Psalms 37:5

At this point, it has been well established that trusting in God is of significant importance in your life, especially when it comes to finances and abundance.

In James 4:13-15 NASB, the Bible says, *"Come now, you who say, 'Today or tomorrow we will go to such and such a city and spend a year there and engage in business and make a profit.' Yet you do not know what your life will be like tomorrow. You are just a vapor that appears for a little while and then vanishes away. Instead, you ought to say, 'If the Lord wills, we will live and also do this or that.'"*

Asking for God's guidance and seeking His plan gives authority to our plans. As an author, I have personally heard people question, "Well who are you to say….?" or "They do not have any authority over this or that…."

The authority and guidance that you should be seeking is that of God and Jesus Christ.

James 3:17- 18 NASB states, *"But the wisdom from above is first pure, then peaceable, gentle, reasonable, full of mercy and good fruits, unwavering, without hypocrisy. And the seed whose fruit is righteousness is sown in peace by those who make peace."*

Therefore, trusting in God's guidance for setting financial goals will result in goals that are pure, reasonable, unwavering, and will bear fruit. The fruit is the financial abundance gained for God's glory and to expand His Kingdom here on earth.

Proverbs 16:9 NIV reminds us, *"In their hearts humans plan their course, but the Lord establishes their steps."*

By seeking and anchoring your trust in God's guidance, you can find a solid direction for your financial goals. God will speak to you, sometimes in a verse, sometimes in confirmations around you, and Isaiah 30:21 NIV says, *"Whether you turn to the right or to the left, your ears will hear a voice behind you, saying, 'This is the way; walk in it."*

Sometimes, it is that small voice in the back of your head. That is God speaking and guiding you. Trust in it.

"I will instruct you and teach you in the way you should go; I will counsel you with my loving eye on you," Psalms 32:8 NIV.

Faith-Fueled Financial Planning

Faith-fueled financial planning is a powerful approach that intertwines trust in God with our financial decisions. As you embark on this journey of stewardship and financial responsibility, you can find solace in Proverbs 3:5 NIV, which urges you to *"Trust in the Lord with all your heart and lean not on your own understanding."*

This trust is not blind; it is rooted in faith. Our faith propels us to commit our financial endeavors to the Lord, as Proverbs 16:3 NIV advises, *"Commit to the Lord whatever you do, and he will establish your plans."*

In this approach, you should recognize that your financial resources are ultimately God's, and your role is to be faithful stewards.

As you embrace generosity, guided by Luke 6:38, which promises abundance for those who give, you witness the transformative impact of faith-fueled financial planning not only in your lives but also in the lives of others. This approach not only secures your financial future but also aligns your aspirations with God's divine purpose.

To create a faith-driven financial plan grounded in biblical principles, start by clearly identifying your core values and beliefs about money and personal finances. Establish a foundation for your plan based on biblical concepts and teachings.

Determine how these principles align with your financial goals and decisions, ensuring that your faith guides your approach to managing and stewarding your resources.

You can reflect and ask yourself questions like - Are you planning to be more generous in your giving, setting aside money to make contributions to community charities?

Is stewardship a big part of your financial planning? The sample list of Christian Financial Goals from the God-Inspired Goals section in this chapter covers many topics you may want to consider.

Avoiding unnecessary and excessive debt is good in any financial plan, and as already shown, is a biblical principle as well. Once you have set the values your plan is based on, you will want to set clear financial goals.

Using the SMART method in this book is a fantastic way to clearly define your goals. You may want to consider making several financial goals at the same time. By setting various goals simultaneously, you can address different aspects of your life while enhancing your financial well-being.

Consider establishing short-term goals, such as saving for an upcoming mission trip or a well-deserved vacation. Simultaneously, create long-term goals, like saving for a college education or securing a comfortable retirement.

Perhaps you aspire to move into a new home; remember that personal goals, even those that may seem self-serving, align with God's plans for our lives.

"Build houses and live in them; and plant gardens and eat their produce," Jeremiah 29:5 NASB.

Within your personal desires, you will find God's desires for you and your life.

Continue to seek the answers and God's guidance through prayer for your personal desires.

"You will seek Me and find Me when you search for Me with all your heart. I will be found by you, declares the Lord," Jeremiah 29:14 NASB.

Along with your faith-based goals, you will want to create a detailed budget that aligns with your God-guided goals. Allocate a portion of your income to essential expenses, savings, investments, and charitable giving. When creating your budget, be sure to include a debt management plan.

Evaluate your existing debts and develop a plan to pay them off. There are several effective debt reduction methods, such as the Avalanche method or the Snowball Method.

The Snowball method means paying off your debt in order of smallest balance to most significant balance. In this strategy, once the smallest debt is paid off, you roll that payment over into the next smallest debt.

You keep moving your payments into the next debt picking up, or "snowballing," and the payments get larger and more significant for each debt. This, ideally, keeps going until all debt is paid off.

Your budget stays the same for the entirety of the process, but in the end, you are debt-free. Here is how it works:

> **Step 1:** List your debts from smallest to largest regardless of interest rate.
>
> **Step 2:** Make minimum payments on all your debts except the smallest.
>
> **Step 3:** Pay as much as possible on your smallest debt.
>
> **Step 4:** Repeat until all debts are paid in full.

With this method you prioritize paying off your smallest debt first, regardless of its interest rate.

This approach can provide a sense of achievement and motivation to continue working towards paying off your debts. By following this strategy, you can improve your financial well-being and achieve a debt-free status in the long run.

The Avalanche Method is a debt payment strategy that prioritizes paying off the debt with the highest interest rate first.

As you make payments, you continue to allocate the same amount of money towards the next highest interest debt and so on until all your debts are paid off. By focusing on the interest rate rather than the balance, you can save more money overall and pay off your debt faster.

Whichever method you prefer is a personal choice and should be discussed with a financial consultant to determine which works best for you. I believe that utilizing the Snowball Method can help cultivate a positive mindset of progress and achievement.

This can provide the motivation to stay on track and work towards your end goal with a sense of satisfaction and accomplishment. If you are interested, there is a sample debt snowball form included at the end of this book that you may find useful.

The Bible has something to say regarding managing debt as well.

Proverbs 19:17 NIV encourages responsible lending and borrowing, *"Whoever is kind to the poor lends to the Lord, and he will reward them for what they have done."*

Borrowing with the intention of helping others and fulfilling responsibilities is viewed positively.

Romans 13:7-8 NIV advises, *"Give to everyone what you owe them: If you owe taxes, pay taxes; if revenue, then revenue; if respect, then respect; if honor, then honor. Let no debt remain outstanding, except the continuing debt to love one another, for whoever loves others has fulfilled the law."*

This passage underscores the importance of paying off debts promptly.

Proverbs 17:18 NIV cautions against co-signing loans or becoming a guarantor for someone else's debt, *"One who has no sense shakes hands in pledge and puts up security for a neighbor."*

Co-signing can lead to financial difficulties if the other party defaults. Seeking advice from wise and experienced individuals before making financial decisions, including taking on debt, is wise.

When faced with multiple debts, it is important to prioritize them. Prioritize your debts based on their importance and interest rates. Even when dealing with debt, the Bible encourages generosity and compassion toward others.

Proverbs 28:27 NIV states, *"Those who give to the poor will lack nothing, but those who close their eyes to them receive many curses."*

Consider exploring investment options that are consistent with your faith and values. For example, some religious faiths have guidelines on ethical investing or avoiding investments in certain industries (e.g., alcohol, gambling, etc.)

On matters of investing and portfolios, please seek wise counsel from a financial planner who will honor your faith.

Determine how much of your income you want to allocate to charitable giving or tithing and select causes or organizations that align with your Christian values.

Faith-fueled financial planning also includes building an emergency fund to ensure financial stability during unexpected events. It may not be your own personal emergency event that occurs, but someone else that God leads you to be generous to.

Either way, having an emergency fund to give to those in dire need is an essential part of the planning process. Be sure to periodically review your financial plan to ensure that it remains aligned with your goals and faith-based values.

Adapt your financial plan to any changing circumstances. Again, faith-fueled financial planning is highly personal and should reflect your unique convictions and priorities.

It is imperative to stay true to your faith and God's will for your life while making financial decisions that promote your financial well-being.

Chapter 5: Living a Faith-Driven Financial Life

For many, living a Faith-Driven financial life means making mindful decisions about spending, saving, and investing, with an emphasis on ethical and moral considerations. It often includes giving back to the community through charitable donations and volunteering, as well as living within one's means to avoid excessive debt and financial stress.

Some believe a faith-driven financial life is the pursuit of wealth as not an end in itself but rather a means to support one's family, serve others, and uphold the values and teachings of one's faith.

It is a holistic approach that seeks to bring harmony between one's spiritual and financial well-being, ultimately leading to a more fulfilling and purposeful life.

A faith-driven financial life includes financial decision-making with Christian Values, Honesty, Integrity, and Christian Business Ethics, and Making God-Centered Financial Choices.

Financial Decision-Making with Christian Values

"The Lord detests dishonest scales, but accurate weights find favor with him." Proverbs 11:1 NIV

Making financial decisions guided by Christian values involves a holistic approach to managing money that prioritizes faith, stewardship, and ethical responsibility.

As faithful stewards of God's resources, Christians strive for contentment and avoid excessive debt, recognizing that true wealth lies in godliness.

Budgeting with diligence, giving generously to those in need, and avoiding unethical practices are integral components of this financial ethos.

Ethical investment choices, seeking wise counsel, and planning for the future demonstrate a commitment to responsible financial management.

All of these principles are underpinned by the importance of prayer, trust in God, and the rejection of greed, ensuring that financial decisions not only align with Christian values but also contribute to the well-being of individuals, families, and communities while glorifying God.

Refrain from engaging in dishonest or unethical financial practices, such as fraud, exploitation, or usury (excessive interest rates).

These actions are not in line with Christian values.

Consider ethical and responsible investment options. Proverbs 6:6-8 NIV highlights the importance of planning for the future, *"Go to the ant, you sluggard; consider its ways and be wise! It has no commander, no overseer or ruler, yet it stores its provisions in summer and gathers its food at harvest."*

Save and invest wisely to provide for your family's future needs. Commit your financial decisions to prayer and trust in God's guidance. Guard against the temptation of greed, which can lead to unethical behavior and poor financial decisions.

Luke 12:15 NIV warns, *"Watch out! Be on your guard against all kinds of greed; life does not consist in an abundance of possessions."*

Being accountable for your financial actions involves regularly reviewing your decisions in alignment with your values, seeking guidance through prayer and reflection, involving your family in discussions, and maintaining a trusted accountability partner, ensuring that your choices reflect your ethical and moral principles.

For example, cultivate a relationship with a trusted friend or mentor who shares your values, updating them on your financial journey for guidance and mutual accountability.

This personalized approach ensures that your financial choices reflect not only sound economic principles but also the values that matter most to you and those close to you.

1 Corinthians 4:2 NIV says, *"Now it is required that those who have been given a trust must prove faithful."*

Proverbs 13:11 NIV reminds Christians that *"Dishonest money dwindles away, but whoever gathers money little by little makes it grow."*

Incorporating these principles into your financial decision-making process can help you manage your finances in a way that aligns with Christian values and fosters financial well-being for yourself and others.

Honesty, Integrity, and Christian Business Ethics

Honesty, integrity, and Christian business ethics are the cornerstones of how Christian individuals and organizations navigate the complex landscape of commerce.

Whether you are the owner of a company, or an employee, these values guide every aspect of business endeavors, emphasizing the importance of truthfulness and transparency in all interactions.

You do not have to own a company or be self-employed to be a Christian business leader. Leaders strive to operate with unwavering integrity, adhering to moral and ethical principles even in the face of challenging decisions.

Rooted in the teachings of Christianity, these ethics promote fairness, compassion, and respect for all stakeholders, and align financial success with the principles of faith and righteousness.

If you want to manifest a pay raise at work, to be more financially abundant in your life, but you do not align yourself with Christian business ethics you will encounter difficulty as your actions do not align with God.

These basic values form the foundation of a business approach that seeks to align financial success with moral and spiritual principles.

Honesty is the bedrock of Christian business ethics. It means being truthful and transparent in all business dealings, including communication with customers, other employees, suppliers, and competitors.

Proverbs 22:1 NIV highlights the value of a reputation built on honesty and integrity. *"A good name is more desirable than great riches; to be esteemed is better than silver or gold."*

Christian business owners and leaders are expected to be trustworthy and to fulfill their promises and commitments. Integrity goes hand in hand with honesty and involves adhering to strong moral and ethical principles consistently, even when faced with difficult decisions or temptations.

Christian business ethics prioritize integrity in financial transactions, decision-making, and interactions with stakeholders. This commitment to integrity helps build trust and credibility, fostering long-term relationships with customers and partners.

Proverbs 16:11 NIV emphasizes that God values honesty and fairness in all dealings, *"Honest scales and balances belong to the Lord; all the weights in the bag are of his making."*

Christian business ethics are rooted in the teachings of Christianity, including the Ten Commandments and the teachings of Jesus Christ.

These principles include love, compassion, fairness, and the Golden Rule. (Matthew 7:12 NASB: *"In everything, therefore, treat people the same way you want them to treat you, for this is the Law and the Prophets."*)

Christian business leaders strive to incorporate these values into their business practices, treating others with respect and seeking to do good in the world.

In practical terms, Christian business ethics can manifest in several ways:

Fair Treatment: Treat all employees and stakeholders fairly and equitably, regardless of their background, beliefs, or status.

Charitable Giving: Many Christian businesses allocate a portion of their profits to charitable causes, reflecting their commitment to helping those in need and serving their communities.

Ethical Decision-Making: When faced with ethical dilemmas, Christian business leaders seek guidance from their faith and prayer to make decisions that align with their moral values. Micah 6:8 NIV: *"He has shown you, O mortal, what is good. And what does the Lord require of you? To act justly and to love mercy and to walk humbly with your God."* This verse underscores the importance of ethical behavior and humility.

Accountability: Taking responsibility for one's actions and being accountable for mistakes or wrongdoing is a crucial aspect of Christian business ethics.

Avoiding Exploitation: Ensuring that business practices do not exploit vulnerable individuals or communities and that products and services are produced and marketed ethically.

Christian business ethics further emphasize the idea that business is not just a means of financial gain but also an opportunity to live out one's faith by positively impacting the world and exemplifying Christian values in the marketplace.

Colossians 3:8-10 NIV *"But now you must rid yourselves of all such things as these: anger, rage, malice, slander, and filthy language from your lips. Do not lie to each other, since you have taken off your old self with its practices and have put on the new self, which is being renewed in knowledge in the image of its Creator."*

This verse speaks to the Christian call to truthfulness and transformation.

Matthew 5:16 NIV encourages Christians to set a positive example through their actions. *"In the same way, let your light shine before others, that they may see your good deeds and glorify your Father in heaven."*

The goal is to achieve financial success while maintaining a solid commitment to honesty, integrity, and Christian principles.

Making God-Centered Financial Choices

Embarking on a journey of God-centered financial choices is a deeply personal and spiritually guided expedition. It is not just a set of steps; it is a path that intertwines your faith with the practical aspects of managing your finances.

To kickstart this journey, consider reaching out to a trusted church leader or mentor, someone within your faith community who resonates with your values.

Seek counsel that goes beyond numbers, delving into the spiritual dimensions of financial decision-making. As you navigate this path, let prayer and reflection be your guide.

Take moments to discern how your financial choices can harmonize with your Christian beliefs, weaving a tapestry of values that align with your spiritual compass.

Embrace the profound concept of stewardship, acknowledging that the resources you possess are gifts from God. Your role is to manage your resources wisely, with a sense of responsibility and gratitude.

Remember that Proverbs 16:3 NIV says, *"Commit to the Lord whatever you do, and he will establish your plans."*

Crafting a budget that mirrors your faith-based priorities is a pivotal step. Consider allocating a portion for tithing and supporting charitable causes, recognizing the impact of your financial decisions on the greater good.

Resist the allure of excessive debt and materialism, finding contentment in what you have rather than constantly chasing more.

Let generosity be a cornerstone of your financial journey. Beyond tithing, actively support those in need, extending a helping hand to others in alignment with your Christian values.

When it comes to investing, choose ethical paths that resonate with your faith principles, ensuring that your financial decisions reflect integrity and virtuous intent.

Continual education is key to staying informed about financial matters, so you can make decisions that align with your faith and stand as a testament to your commitment to responsible stewardship.

In essence, making God-centered financial choices is a profound act of honoring your faith while navigating the complexities of managing your financial resources with grace and purpose.

The Bible has verses that offer valuable insights into the biblical perspective on stewardship and giving. They can serve as a source of inspiration and guidance for those seeking to make God-centered financial choices.

Proverbs 3:9-10 NIV: *"Honor the Lord with your wealth, with the first fruits of all your crops; then your barns will be filled to overflowing, and your vats will brim over with new wine."*

Deuteronomy 16:17 NIV: *"Every man shall give as he is able, according to the blessing of the Lord your God which He has given you."*

Proverbs 19:17 NIV: *"Whoever is kind to the poor lends to the Lord, and he will reward them for what they have done."*

Choose to do business with Christian individuals and businesses. The Bible offers warnings against pursuing wealth through dishonest or get-rich-quick schemes.

Proverbs 20:21 NIV warns *"An inheritance claimed too soon will not be blessed at the end."*

One of the strongest warnings is against falling into temptation and the love of money is in 1 Timothy 6:9-10 NIV *"Those who want to get rich fall into temptation and a trap and into many foolish and harmful desires that plunge people into ruin and destruction. For the love of money is a root of all kinds of evil. Some people, eager for money, have wandered from the faith and pierced themselves with many griefs."*

Do not be deceived by the love of money or the dangle of wealth and riches disguised in schemes.

"A faithful person will be richly blessed, but one eager to get rich will not go unpunished," Proverbs 28:20 NIV.

These verses caution against the pursuit of wealth through dishonest or unethical means, as well as the dangers of greed and impatience in financial matters.

Proverbs 28:22 NIV says, *"The stingy are eager to get rich and are unaware that poverty awaits them."*

Remember to keep your eyes on God, staying focused on making God-centered financial decisions.

Chapter 6: Building Wealth Through Biblical Wisdom

In a world inundated with quick-fix financial advice, the Scriptures offer a unique perspective—one rooted in enduring principles that stand the test of time.

While the Bible may not lay out a step-by-step blueprint for wealth-building akin to modern financial self-help books, its pages are rich with principles that transcend the ages. It speaks to the essence of hard work and diligence, echoing a sentiment captured in Proverbs 10:4 NIV: *"Lazy hands make for poverty, but diligent hands bring wealth."*

Here, you will examine a scriptural approach to managing your finances—a roadmap that begins with living within your means, embracing the discipline of saving, and steering clear of the pitfalls of excessive debt.

But building wealth is not just about avoiding financial pitfalls; it is a journey of gradual accumulation and strategic investment.

As Proverbs 13:11 NIV imparts, *"Wealth gained hastily will dwindle, but whoever gathers little by little will increase it."*

This chapter unfolds the steps to gather that wealth, emphasizing the importance of investing wisely, applying biblical principles to wealth accumulation, and aligning with God's prosperity plan for believers.

So, as we embark on this chapter together, let us explore the intersection of faith and finance, unraveling the threads of biblical wisdom that guide us toward a prosperous and purposeful financial future—one step at a time.

Patience is the key in gaining biblical wealth, and at times it may seem difficult and too far in the distance.

Hebrews 12:11 NIV says, *"No discipline seems pleasant at the time, but painful. Later on, however, it produces a harvest of righteousness and peace for those who have been trained by it."*

Building wealth should not be the sole focus of any person's life, and biblical principles on finances should be balanced with other important aspects of faith, such as compassion, humility, and service to others.

Additionally, individual financial situations can vary, so it is essential to seek guidance and make decisions that align with your specific circumstances and beliefs.

"For to everyone who has, more shall be given, and he will have an abundance; but from the one who does not have, even what he does have shall be taken away," Matthew 25:29 NASB.

Investing with Wisdom and Prudence

If you have ever taken the time to explore the teachings of the Bible, you probably noticed it does not spell out specific investment advice, but it does stress the importance of wise planning.

Now, when it comes to investing, there is a common tendency among many, maybe even yourself, to delay or avoid it for various reasons. Some might think they do not have the financial means, believing a hefty sum is necessary to kickstart an investment account. Others may choose to put off investing until a later stage in life when they anticipate having more disposable income or under different circumstances.

Here is the thing: the earlier you start putting money into your investment accounts, the greater the potential for future wealth.

It is a concept that goes beyond just financial wisdom; it is about actively shaping your financial future.

Despite any strong beliefs you might have about investing later, it is essential to reflect on whether these beliefs are inadvertently contributing to missed opportunities and financial setbacks. Taking a closer look at your mindset could be the key to unlocking greater financial success.

One example that financialfreedom.com uses is if you start with nothing in an account and you budget to invest $2,000 a year for thirty (30) years, you have approximately $328,988 in the account.

If you wait just ten (10) years to start investing the same money, you will only have $114,550.

By waiting and procrastinating, you forfeited $214,450.

The Bible warns of procrastination in Ecclesiastes 11:4 NIV *"Whoever watches the wind will not plant; whoever looks at the clouds will not reap."*

Do not just ask God to bless you financially then do nothing but stare at the clouds, take effective action.

Once you begin investing most financial advisors suggest having a diversified portfolio.

Ecclesiastes 11:2 NIV suggests diversifying investments: *"Invest in seven ventures, yes, in eight; you do not know what disaster may come upon the land."*

Investing in different types of assets will minimize your risk, thereby protecting your investments. When you have your money spread through different investments, you are also giving God different avenues to bless you financially.

Remember when you are manifesting through God's guidance and His abundance, you need to be prudent and not box God into one way or another. Allow His abundance to flow through many sources, including financial investments.

When it comes to managing your investments, I want to emphasize the importance of tapping into the wisdom of financial experts. Consider reaching out to individuals within your community and church who have experience in financial investing.

By doing so, you not only benefit from their knowledge but also contribute to the prosperity of others in the Kingdom of God.

Imagine the impact when your investments become a source of support for someone in your local church who works as an investment broker.

Your money does not just grow in a portfolio; it becomes a lifeline for a fellow Christian striving to keep their business afloat.

This creates a beautiful cycle of communal support, where your financial endeavors contribute to the well-being of your faith community. Moreover, as you embark on your investment journey, prioritize ethical choices that align with your Christian principles. Select companies that reflect your values, ensuring that your investments are not only financially sound but also morally grounded.

This way, you are not just growing your wealth but also investing in a manner that resonates with your deeply held beliefs.

In essence, the act of investing transcends mere financial transactions; it becomes a meaningful way to connect with your community, support fellow believers, and uphold your Christian values in the world of finance.

Honor God with your wealth. Proverbs 3:9-10 NIV advises, *"Honor the Lord with your wealth, with the first fruits of all your crops; then your barns will be filled to overflowing, and your vats will brim over with new wine."*

Many believe that dedicating a portion of their income to religious or charitable purposes can bring blessings.

"Freely you have received; freely give," Matthew 10:8 NIV.

If there is only one principle you get from this book, it should be this: God desires to provide Christian's with abundance and wealth so that they may give.

Biblical Investing is not solely about padding your personal accounts with wealth. It is about using material wealth to further God's Kingdom here on earth.

The more you have, the more you give, the more you will abundantly receive.

Biblical Principles for Wealth Accumulation

Embarking on the journey of wealth accumulation rooted in biblical principles brings a deeply personal understanding of how God views material prosperity. It is a recognition that every facet of our lives, be it money, wealth, land, or possessions, is ultimately a gift from the divine.

As Psalms 24:1 NIV reminds us, *"The earth is the Lord's, and everything in it, the world, and all who live in it."*

This foundational truth transforms our approach to wealth, prompting us to see ourselves as stewards entrusted with God's resources.

In embracing these principles, the focus shifts from mere financial pursuits to a full understanding that every possession and provision is a tangible expression of God's grace.

This wisdom invites us to toil with purpose and, equally importantly, to share generously with those in need. It is a personal journey of aligning our financial endeavors with the enduring principles laid out in the Scriptures, recognizing that true wealth is found not just in accumulation but in the joyful stewardship of God's abundant blessings.

In the first part of this book the example of the homeless man highlighted the idea to change how you view the money as it goes out of your hand.

In the same thought, blessing the money, no matter to the perception of the person's use of it, but blessing it knowing that God will use it for the purpose He has destined it for.

If you lose money in some form or fashion, be it you dropped a twenty-dollar bill on the ground, or there is a recession and you lose money in your investments, bless it as it goes out.

Bless the money knowing God is ultimately in control of its end destination.

Remember, it is the love of money that is evil, not the money itself.

"He who loves money will not be satisfied with money, nor he who loves abundance with its income. This too is vanity," Ecclesiastes 5:10 NASB.

Recognize money for what it is—an ephemeral butterfly that flits through our lives. It is essential not to succumb to despair when faced with financial setbacks, for such feelings often stem from an excessive love of money itself.

When we become fixated on the material, our gaze shifts away from the divine plan that God has intricately woven for our lives. If negative emotions surround money, it serves as a crucial signal that we may have momentarily lost sight of God's purpose—to bless and build.

In those moments of financial turbulence, consider it an opportunity to recalibrate your focus and rekindle the awareness of God's greater design. Letting go of the fleeting butterfly of money allows us to open our hands to receive the more enduring blessings that God has in store.

It is a personal journey of trust, acknowledging that God's plan encompasses far more than fleeting financial gains or losses, and finding peace in the assurance that His purpose for your life goes beyond the transient nature of wealth.

Go back to the drawing board and use the Manifestation P.R.A.Y.E.R.™ method, really seeking what your true desires and intentions are.

The passage in 1 Kings 3:10-13 regarding Solomon and his request for discernment in justice is an amazing biblical principle regarding our focus in wealth accumulation.

God honored that Solomon did not come seeking riches or a long life. Solomon did not request any vengeance toward his enemies. Instead, he asked for discernment and God honored his request, and then some.

"It was pleasing in the sight of the Lord that Solomon had asked this thing. God said to him, 'Because you have asked this thing and have not asked for yourself long life, nor have asked riches for yourself, nor have you asked for the life of your enemies, but have asked for yourself discernment to understand justice, behold, I have done according to your words. Behold, I have given you a wise and discerning heart, so that there has been no one like you before you, nor shall one like you arise after you. I have also given you what you have not asked, both in riches and honor, so that there will not be any among the kings like you all your days."

In verse 13 God says, *"I have also given you what you have not asked, both riches and honor...."*

God deeply values the desires and intentions within your heart, especially when your aim is to amass wealth for the explicit purpose of advancing His Kingdom.

As you embark on this personal journey, take a moment to sincerely seek His guidance and discernment. Specifically, ask for the wisdom to generously contribute to the well-being of your community and the growth of your church.

When your aspirations align with God's purpose, you will uncover a wellspring of wisdom sourced directly from Him. In this intimate pursuit, rest assured that God's response goes beyond a mere reward—it is a personal honor tailored to your unique journey.

Trust in His divine guidance, and you will witness His blessings unfolding in ways that exceed your wildest imagination. It is a deeply personal and fulfilling connection, where your efforts resonate with a sense of purpose, contributing not only to your own prosperity but also to the profound impact of God's Kingdom here on Earth.

"Your dreams need to be bigger than you can imagine so that God can be involved." - Unknown

The idea of dreaming of wealth beyond our imagination in order for God to get involved reflects a perspective of faith and trust in divine intervention. It suggests that by having audacious, ambitious financial dreams that go beyond the limits of the human imagination, opens the door for the possibility of God's blessing.

"The blessing of the Lord brings wealth, without painful toil for it," Proverbs 10:22 NIV.

Many people believe that when they set lofty goals and dreams, they are aligning themselves with a higher purpose or calling, and in doing so, they may receive inspiration from God, along with opportunities to help them achieve these dreams.

It is a way of acknowledging that God's involvement can be a catalyst for achieving extraordinary wealth.

Proverbs 3:5-6 NIV says, *"Trust in the Lord with all your heart and lean not on your own understanding; in all your ways submit to Him, and He will make your paths straight."*

This again reminds Christians to rely on God's wisdom, believing that He will lead us on the right path.

God's Prosperity Plan for Believers

The concept of "God's prosperity plan" in the Bible is often associated with passages that talk about God's blessings, provision, and abundance.

While the Bible does contain verses that emphasize prosperity, it is essential to consider these passages in their broader context and the various interpretations they can have.

Jeremiah 29:11 NIV: *"For I know the plans I have for you, declares the Lord, plans for welfare and not for evil, to give you a future and a hope."*

This verse is often cited to emphasize God's plans for the well-being and prosperity of his people. When discussing God's prosperity, it is important to focus on His view and purpose.

God desires that you use your prosperity to honor Him, more than just to gain material possessions to make your lives better.

The Parable of the Sower is a fitting example of God's plan for prosperity.

Matthew 12:3-17 NASB: *"Then he told them many things in parables, saying: 'A farmer went out to sow his seed. As he was scattering the seed, some fell along the path, and the birds came and ate it up. Some fell on rocky places, where it did not have much soil. It sprang up quickly because the soil was shallow. But when the sun came up, the plants were scorched, and they withered because they had no root. Other seed fell among thorns, which grew up and choked the plants. Still other seed fell on good soil, where it produced a crop—a hundred, sixty or thirty times what was sown. Whoever has ears, let them hear.'"*

The disciples came to him and asked, 'Why do you speak to the people in parables?'

He replied, "Because the knowledge of the secrets of the kingdom of heaven has been given to you, but not to them. Whoever has will be given more, and they will have an abundance. Whoever does not have, even what they have will be taken from them. This is why I speak to them in parables:

"Though seeing, they do not see; though hearing, they do not hear or understand. In them is fulfilled the prophecy of Isaiah: 'You will be ever hearing but never understanding; you will be ever seeing but never perceiving. For this people's heart has become calloused; they hardly hear with their ears, and they have closed their eyes. Otherwise, they might see with their eyes, hear with their ears, understand with their hearts, and turn, and I would heal them.'

But blessed are your eyes because they see, and your ears because they hear. For truly I tell you, many prophets and righteous people longed to see what you see but did not see it, and to hear what you hear but did not hear it.

"Listen then to what the parable of the Sower means: When anyone hears the message about the kingdom and does not understand it, the evil one comes and snatches away what was sown in their heart. This is the seed sown along the path. The seed falling on rocky ground refers to someone who hears the word and at once receives it with joy. But since they have no root, they last only a short time.

"When trouble or persecution comes because of the word, they quickly fall away. The seed falling among the thorns refers to someone who hears the word, but the worries of this life and the deceitfulness of wealth choke the word, making it unfruitful. But the seed falling on good soil refers to someone who hears the word and understands it. This is the one who produces a crop, yielding a hundred, sixty or thirty times what was sown."

Simplifying the parable, if you sew in good soil, you will reap many times beyond what you have sown.

Financially speaking, let us delve into the heart of God's Prosperity Plan—a blueprint that begins with an earnest pursuit of God Himself.

Matthew 6:33 NIV, a cornerstone of this plan, nudges us to prioritize the search for God's kingdom and righteousness: *"But seek first his kingdom and his righteousness, and all these things will be given to you as well."*

Colossians 3:2 NASB, echoes this sentiment, urging us to fix our gaze on the celestial rather than the terrestrial: *"Set your mind on the things above, not on the things that are on earth."*

Discovering the heart of God's Prosperity Plan is like embarking on a profound journey. It does not begin with self-sufficiency, but with a purposeful quest for God Himself.

Picture this: as you navigate the complex path towards financial well-being, the very foundation is established by surrendering to the One who not only knows your needs but is also able to extravagantly meet them as you walk hand in hand with Him, harmonizing with His divine purpose.

It is a special moment when your dreams meet the endless grace of God.

The second part of God's Prosperity Plan is to sow your seeds in the good soil of His word, the Bible, just as Jesus highlighted in The Parable of the Sower.

When you use the teachings and principles all throughout the Bible to use your money wisely and invest properly into God's Kingdom you will be prosperous.

"But his delight is in the law of the Lord, And in His law he meditates day and night. He will be like a tree firmly planted by streams of water, which yields its fruit in its season and its leaf does not wither; And in whatever he does, he prospers," Psalms 1:2-3 NASB.

Notice that this verse speaks of meditating day and night on the law of the Lord (the soil again).

Jesus shows believers in the parable of the Sower that you already know the secret to prosperity, *"He replied, 'Because the knowledge of the secrets of the kingdom of heaven has been given to you, but not to them. Whoever has will be given more, and they will have an abundance,'"* Matthew 13:11-12 NIV.

Further into the explanation of the parable to the disciples Jesus says, *"But the seed falling on good soil refers to someone who hears the word and understands it. This is the one who produces a crop, yielding a hundred, sixty or thirty times what was sown,"* Matthew 13:23 NIV.

Jesus is teaching that you are already abundant because you have been given the word of God. You have a secret better than any riches out there. You then know without doubt that when you use the word of God, following all the teachings, God will bless you with prosperity.

To truly honor and glorify God, as a believer you are urged to integrate daily prayer and meditation into your daily life.

This practice, constituting the third crucial element of God's Prosperity Plan, encourages a profound connection with the divine through the deliberate reflection on biblical wisdom.

Infuse your prayers with gratitude, acknowledging God's provisions and cultivating a mindset of thankfulness for what you already possess.

A key lesson on prayer, as imparted by Jesus in John 15:7 NASB, *"If you abide in Me, and My words abide in you, ask whatever you wish, and it will be done for you,"* emphasizes seeking your desires through prayerful communion with God rather than relying solely on self, promising prosperity through this divine connection.

Throughout this book, the significance of gratitude has been explored, from fostering a thankful mindset to appreciating existing blessings.

This theme holds a prominent position in God's Prosperity Plan, echoing the sentiments of 1 Thessalonians 5:16-18 NIV, *"Rejoice always, pray continually, give thanks in all circumstances; for this is God's will for you in Christ Jesus."*

These words serve as a perpetual reminder of the intricate dance between prayer, gratitude, and God's intended prosperity for your life.

The next step in God's Prosperity Plan for you as a Christian involves putting in dedicated effort. Relying solely on prayer, positive thoughts, and scripture might seem appealing, but it is not enough and could be seen as a passive approach.

While maintaining a positive attitude and having faith in your goals are crucial, it is equally vital to translate that faith into action by taking practical steps towards achieving them.

This active engagement aligns with God's design for your prosperity, combining spiritual principles with the tangible efforts you invest in your journey.

As a matter of fact, the Bible says, *"Wealth gotten by vanity shall be diminished: But he that gathereth by labor shall increase,"* Proverbs 13:11 KJV.

God instructs you to work for your money, and not expect wealth to be handed to you.

The Bible also states in Proverbs 10:4 NIV, *"Lazy hands make for poverty, but diligent hands bring wealth,"* and in 2 Thessalonians 3:10 NIV, *"For even when we were with you, we gave you this rule: 'The one who is unwilling to work shall not eat."*

God's Prosperity Plan includes working and effectively taking action to acquire the wealth God plans in your life.

Hebrews 6:12 NIV incorporates working with having patience. *"We do not want you to become lazy, but to imitate those who through faith and patience inherit what has been promised."*

Having patience and trusting in His timing is the next step in God's Prosperity Plan. "Patience is a virtue." You have more than likely heard this many times in your life.

My grandmother had a phrase she repeated often, "Lord, give me patience and give it to me now." Of course, this is a funny way of acknowledging impatience.

God requires trust in His timing as discussed in Chapter 4, Psalms 27:14 NIV charges you to *"Wait for the Lord; be strong and take heart and wait for the Lord."*

This is a powerful instruction from God to wait on Him and his timing.

"Trust in the Lord and do good; Dwell in the land and cultivate faithfulness. Delight yourself in the Lord; and He will give you the desires of your heart," Psalms 37:3-4 NASB.

God's promise to you is to trust in Him, and He will give you the desires of your heart.

The most important of God's Prosperity Plan is when God prospers us, we should be generous in giving to those in need and walk by the Spirit.

Paul wrote in Galatians 5:14 NASB, *"For the whole Law is fulfilled in one word, in the statement, 'You shall love your neighbor as yourself.'"*

It is your responsibility to love everyone, help the less fortunate in your community, and grow the Kingdom of God. Those who are less fortunate will see the Spirit working through you, and God will bless that.

"One who is gracious to a poor man lends to the Lord, and He will repay him for his good deed," Proverbs 19:17 NASB.

The last part of God's Prosperity Plan is pure belief and to bear witness of the glory of God.

Belief in God, belief in His Provision, belief in the will of God. You must believe in God to inherit the greatest abundance that exists, eternal life. God wants to be manifested through you and for you.

"But he who practices the truth comes to the Light, so that his deeds may be manifested as having been wrought in God," John 3:21 NASB.

The greatest testimony in manifesting prosperity through God's Prosperity Plan is that God is manifest through you.

Romans 12:2 NASB states, *"And do not be conformed to this world, but be transformed by the renewing of your mind, so that you may prove what the will of God is, that which is good and acceptable and perfect."*

The greatest and final part of God's Prosperity Plan is not for personal gain and wealth, but for you to proclaim the glory of God so that you may bring many nations into the Kingdom of God.

Jesus instructed in John 15:16 NIV, *"You did not choose me, but I chose you and appointed you so that you might go and bear fruit – fruit that will last – and so that whatever you ask in my name the Father will give you.*

God's Prosperity Plan – A Quick Outline:
1. *Seek First God's kingdom and Righteousness* (Matthew 6:33, Colossians 3:1, Luke 12:30-31)
2. *Sow your seeds in good soil – invest properly and use money wisely based on biblical principles.* (Matthew 13:1-23, Psalms 1:1-3)
3. *Meditate and pray, and in all things, give thanks to God.* (John 15:7, 1 Thessalonians 5:18)
4. *Work diligently – Do not be lazy and expect God to just answer you without any effort* (Proverbs 10:4, Proverbs 13:11, 2 Thessalonians 3:10)
5. *Have patience and trust in God's timing.* (Hebrews 6:12, Psalms 27:14, Psalms 37:3-4)
6. *Give back to the Kingdom of God.* (Galatians 5:14 – 22, Proverbs 19:17)
7. *Pure Belief and be a witness for God's Prosperity Plan* (John 3:21, Romans 12:2, and John 15:16)

It is important to approach these verses with a balanced perspective. While they offer a guideline for prosperity, they are not a guarantee of financial or material wealth.

Prosperity in the biblical context is often understood as not only material wealth but also spiritual well-being, peace, and living in alignment with God's will.

Additionally, the context of each verse and the surrounding passages should be considered when seeking to understand their full meaning.

Fully plant your beliefs and your desires in the Bible and God's word (the good soil), meditate and pray on it, ask from a place of growing the Kingdom of God not for personal gain, and you will prosper.

Chapter 7: Handling Financial Challenges with Faith

Christian faith is a powerful compass that guides us through life's storms, including financial challenges. When facing economic hardships, turning to your spiritual beliefs can provide a source of strength and resilience.

Through prayer, meditation, and the support of our faith communities, you find solace, guidance, and a reminder that you are not alone in your struggles.

Our faith teaches us to be responsible stewards of our finances, promoting wise management and patience in times of scarcity. It instills in you a deep sense of gratitude for the blessings you do have and encourages acts of charity, even when our own resources are limited.

Above all, faith inspires us to trust in God and remain patient, knowing that, in time, our financial burdens can be lightened through resilience, guidance, and a sense of purpose.

Isaiah 41:10 NIV says, *"So do not fear, for I am with you; do not be dismayed, for I am your God. I will strengthen you and help you; I will uphold you with my righteous right hand."*

Finding strength in God during financial crises is a testament to the resilience of one's beliefs. Overcoming debt and financial struggles can be a spiritual journey where trust in God becomes a foundation to lean upon.

Trusting God's provision in times of need, with faith and perseverance, you can find solutions and hope in the face of adversity. In the midst of financial uncertainty, leaning on one's faith can provide the emotional and spiritual support needed to navigate these challenges and emerge with renewed strength and a deepened connection to one's beliefs.

Moreover, everyone's faith and beliefs are personal, so the way in which faith is used to address financial challenges can vary greatly from person to person. It is essential to find what works best for you and aligns with your beliefs and values.

Finding Strength in God During Financial Crises

"Be strong and courageous. Do not be afraid or terrified because of them, for the Lord your God goes with you; He will never leave you nor forsake you." Deuteronomy 31:6 NIV

Back in 1999, as a divorced single mother with two small children, I was struggling financially. I was too prideful to ask my parents for any help.

I worked as a receptionist, barely making over minimum wage. I had no idea how I was going to pay my bills, specifically my mortgage of $750 at the time.

With childcare costs eating up most of my money, I was sinking quickly. Now, let me remind you that in 1999, most things were still done via the postal service. We did not have smartphones – we had flip phones that you did not dare use because you would be charged by the minute if you used them.

At the time, I was not paying for my cell phone because it was still on my grandparents-in-law's phone bill. Which gave me pause to use the phone that much more.

I remember sitting on the floor in my living room with all the bills spread out around me. My paper checkbook in hand, balancing the register while budgeting out to the penny for childcare, gas to get to work, fifty dollars for groceries, the power bill, and the water bill.

I did not have enough money for the mortgage, nor did I have any money left for anything extra or frivolous.

I remember looking up at the vaulted ceiling in my living room and praying to God. I felt so overwhelmed by it all. I stared at the white swirls in the ceiling plaster and decided then and there I was going to just let it go and give it over to God.

I prayed from a thankful heart that I had a roof over my head. I thanked God that I did not have a car payment. I praised Him that I was always taken care of no matter what was going on in my life. I expressed true, heartfelt gratitude and love for my all-knowing and loving God.

I said something to the effect of, "God, I just ask that you somehow keep this roof over our heads. I give it all to you and believe you will take care of us."

I repeated a Bible verse I had heard most of my life back to God.

Matthew 6:26 NIV, *"Look at the birds of the air; they do not sow or reap or store away in barns, and yet your heavenly Father feeds them. Are you not much more valuable than they?"*

Of course, I paraphrased it as something like, "God, you take care of the birds in the air, and your word says I am more valuable; please hear my prayers."

My mortgage was due in a week, and I had no idea what to do, where the money would come from, or how I was going to pay it. But I left it in God's capable hands.

Two days before the rent was due, after working a full day, I pulled into the driveway and stopped at the mailbox like I always did. I felt tired and drained. I had not given the mortgage another thought, as I had truly given the issue over to God.

I did not feel irresponsible in my thinking, as I just had pure faith in God.

I brought the kids into the house and pulled something out of the refrigerator to make for dinner. I called my mother, as I did most days, and spoke to her while I was cooking at the stove.

I saw the pile of mail on the counter, and I remember feeling almost sick to my stomach, like I just did not want to face the looming bills.

I finished the call with my mother and then set my kids at the table to eat. I stood in the middle of the kitchen while the kids were eating and just took a deep breath.

Again, I just asked God to please help me.

I had not been irresponsible with my money, I was good at keeping up with my bills, and I did not have too much debt outside of the normal expenses. I had always been faithful in giving money to others when they needed it if I had extra. I once paid for a friend's phone bill when she was strapped for cash just so she had a way to communicate with anyone if she needed to. I gave shelter generously with my home and money to anyone in need.

I picked up the top piece of mail; the weight of it felt slightly heavier than a normal bill or letter. I haphazardly ripped open the envelope, finding a brand new, shiny blue credit card.

I had applied for a credit card weeks earlier via the mail, then promptly forgot about it. In 1999, unlike today, you filled out a form, placed a stamp on it, then mailed it in.

Many times, waiting weeks to find out if you were approved or not, one could always call to see if you were approved, but I had not done that.

I opened the folded paper slowly, reading the words: "Congratulations! You have been approved for a credit limit of $2,500!"

Tears streamed down my face as I realized my prayers were fully answered. I fully let go and gave my financial situation over to God, and He gave me more than I needed. I was able to pay the mortgage and have a little freedom in between paychecks when bills were due, or childcare needed to be paid.

I became very diligent in paying off anything I charged on the card during that time. This began my journey of always trusting God that I would be taken care of.

More importantly, it was the first time the framework of my financial prayers was crystal clear to me.

Earlier in this book, the steps were outlined in the Manifestation PRAYER. Those same steps I have used since 1999 always helped me when I faced financial struggles.

To say that God has shown me over and over His grace and taken care of my needs is an understatement.

Today, I live in a very exclusive condominium complex with all the amenities. I have a nice car, money in my retirement, savings in my bank, food in my house, and bills that are paid, and I am a successfully published author.

My needs and my desires are met all the time.

Psalms 23 is a passage that I rely on in times that may be tough or when financial needs arise.

A Psalm of David.

23 The Lord is my shepherd,
I shall not want.
2 He makes me lie down in green pastures;
He leads me beside quiet waters.
3 He restores my soul;

He guides me in the paths of righteousness
For His name's sake.
⁴ Even though I walk through the valley of the shadow of death,
I fear no evil, for You are with me;
Your rod and Your staff, they comfort me.
⁵ You prepare a table before me in the presence of my enemies;
You have anointed my head with oil;
My cup overflows.
⁶ Surely goodness and lovingkindness will follow me all the days of my life,
And I will dwell in the house of the Lord forever.

Overcoming Debt and Financial Struggles

Overcoming debt and financial struggles can be a daunting challenge, but with determination, discipline, and a well-thought-out plan, it is possible to improve your financial situation.

Overcoming debt and financial struggles is a demanding yet achievable endeavor with the right mindset and strategy. It begins with a comprehensive assessment of your financial situation, understanding your debts, income, and expenses.

Setting clear and attainable God-centered financial goals helps you stay focused on your journey to stability.

James 1:5 NIV says, *"If any of you lacks wisdom, you should ask God, who gives generously to all without finding fault, and it will be given to you."*

Ask for God's guidance when setting your financial goals.

Crafting a well-structured budget is pivotal; it enables you to prioritize essential expenses while redirecting funds toward debt reduction.

Negotiating with creditors, building an emergency fund, and finding ways to increase your income can provide invaluable assistance along the way.

As you navigate this process, remember that it is not just about the destination but also the journey – every step taken, no matter how small, is a victory worth celebrating.

With commitment and support from professionals, mentors, or loved ones, you can surmount financial challenges, achieve debt freedom, and pave the way for a more financially secure future.

"God is our refuge and strength, an ever-present help in trouble," Psalms 46:1 NIV.

Here are some steps to help you on your journey to financial stability:

Assess Your Situation: Begin by taking a close look at your financial circumstances. Understand the extent of your debt, your income, and your expenses. Create a detailed budget to track your financial inflow and outflow.

Set Realistic Goals: Establish clear, achievable financial goals. Whether it is reducing your debt, increasing your savings, or both, having specific objectives will give you direction.

Create a Budget: Develop a budget that aligns with your financial goals. Allocate your income to cover essential expenses like housing, utilities, groceries, and debt repayment. Cut out unnecessary expenses and redirect funds toward debt reduction.

Prioritize Debt Payment: Identify high-interest debts, such as credit card balances, and focus on paying them down first. Make minimum payments on other debts while aggressively tackling the high-interest ones. Try using the Snowball or Avalanche debt reduction methods.

Seek Professional Advice: If your debt situation is particularly complex or overwhelming, consider consulting with a financial counselor or debt management agency. They can help you develop a structured plan.

Negotiate with Creditors: If you are struggling to meet your debt obligations, contact your creditors to discuss your situation. They may be willing to negotiate lower interest rates, smaller monthly payments, or debt settlement arrangements.

Emergency Fund: While managing debt is a priority, it is also essential to build an emergency fund. Having savings to cover unexpected expenses can prevent you from accumulating more debt during financial crises.

Increase Income: Explore ways to increase your income, such as taking on a part-time job, freelancing, or selling unused items. The extra income can accelerate your debt payoff.

Lifestyle Adjustments: Temporarily make lifestyle adjustments, such as cutting non-essential expenses, until your financial situation stabilizes. This might include dining out less, reducing entertainment costs, and finding more cost-effective alternatives.

Stay Committed: Overcoming financial struggles takes time and persistence. Remain committed to your financial goals and stay disciplined in managing your finances.

Celebrate Small Wins: Acknowledge and celebrate your progress, even if it is small. This will help you stay motivated and maintain a positive attitude.

Maintain a Support System: Share your financial journey with a trusted friend, mentor, or family member who can provide emotional support and encouragement. If your church offers a debt management or financial abundance class, enroll in it so you have a place of support in church as well.

Remember that overcoming debt and financial challenges is a gradual process. It may require sacrifice and discipline, but with time and effort, you can improve your financial situation and build a more secure future.

Trusting God's Provision in Times of Need

"For we live by faith, not by sight." 2 Corinthians 5:7 NIV

Trusting in God's provision during times of need is an act of faith that involves surrendering your worries and concerns to God, believing that He will provide for your needs, and finding solace in His guidance.

Psalm 23:1 NIV says, *"The Lord is my shepherd, I lack nothing."* This trust can be nurtured through prayer, gratitude, and the study of the Bible, which offers reassurance and a sense of divine care.

Hebrews 11:1 NIV speaks of this assurance, *"Now faith is confidence in what we hope for and assurance about what we do not see."*

Waiting for God's timing, active stewardship, and a supportive religious community can help you navigate the challenges you face, but at the same time, you have to posture yourself to receive blessings.

Practicing trust and patience, accepting blessings in unexpected ways, and maintaining hope can also help you find strength and resilience in your spiritual journey.

The story of the first-time gambler is a reminder to trust in God's provision and to keep your eyes on God instead of your own doing.

One Sunday morning, an old farmer stood at the door of the church he had attended his entire life, wearing overalls and a flannel shirt, with his head down.

The pastor saw him and walked towards him with a smile, asking what was bothering him. The farmer looked up with a guilty expression and said, "I'm not good, Preacher. I have committed the worst sin."

The pastor asked him if he wanted to talk about it after the service, and the farmer nodded, proceeding to his regular seat in the pew.

After the service, the farmer stayed seated with his head bowed down. When the last churchgoer left the church, the pastor sat down quietly next to the farmer and waited for a few moments before speaking.

"Do you want to talk about it now?" he asked.

The farmer looked up, fixed his eyes on the cross at the front of the church, and said, "Preacher, I went to Vegas."

The pastor patted the farmer on his shoulder, relieved that it was not something worse, and said, "God forgives all things. I'm sure you going to Vegas is forgivable in God's eyes. Did you gamble?"

The pastor surmised this was the big issue.

"Yeah, but that is not the worst part. You see, I decided to go to Vegas just to say I had been there. I did not think I would partake in much of the sinnin' goin' on. But as I got into my hotel and headed to my room, I saw this shiny slot machine next to the elevator. I got a wild hair, I put a twenty-dollar bill in it, and I won ten thousand dollars," the farmer explained.

The pastor's eyes opened wide. "What did you do?" he asked curiously.

"I went to my room and went to bed," replied the farmer plainly.

The surprised pastor, trying to find what would make the farmer so upset, said, "Good for you. I am sure God will forgive you for this."

"Preacher, that's not all," the farmer continued, "The next morning I came downstairs and saw the same shiny slot machine by the elevator. I put another twenty-dollar bill in the machine."

"And you lost it?" the pastor interrupted.

"No sir," replied the farmer. "I won another ten thousand dollars."

The pastor was now completely shocked. He pulled a handkerchief from his pocket and wiped the beading sweat from his forehead.

"Is this when you decided to come home?"

"No, see this is where I got me some courage," the farmer said.

The pastor, believing the farmer felt guilt over winning all that money, said, "I know that God will forgive you. The Bible reminds us it is the love of money that is evil. It is okay that you have the money, as long as you are prudent with it."

"No, I got me some courage then I went gambling and lost it all," the farmer continued.

"I felt 'I' could win. I took my eyes off of God for a while and I lost it all."

You see, the farmer was not feeling remorse about losing the money or gambling. He felt guilty because he took his eyes off of God, believing he was more capable. God's provision will always be more than you could ever do on your own.

The Bible is a wellspring of wisdom and guidance when it comes to trusting in God's provision. It is filled with stories of individuals who faced seemingly insurmountable challenges but found their way through faith and trust in God's promises.

The narratives of Abraham, Joseph, Daniel, and David, among others, are tales of resilience in the face of adversity, all underpinned by unwavering faith.

As mentioned at the beginning of this chapter, Hebrews 11:1 reminds us that faith is about confidence in what you hope for and assurance in what you cannot see. This verse emphasizes the importance of trust even when circumstances appear uncertain. It is about believing that God's plan is unfolding, even if it is not immediately evident.

Prayer is the cornerstone of nurturing trust in God's provision.

It is a direct line of communication with the divine, a channel through which you can pour out your hopes, fears, and aspirations.

In your moments of need, prayer allows you to acknowledge that you are not alone in facing life's challenges. It is an expression of your trust that God is listening and will answer in His way and time.

But prayer is not just about asking for help; it is also about expressing gratitude for the blessings you have received.

When you are aware of these past provisions, it becomes easier to trust that He will continue to do so in the future.

Ephesians 3:20 NASB reminds you that God provides more abundantly than you ask for or think about. *"Now to Him who is able to do far more abundantly beyond all that we ask or think, according to the power that works within us, to Him be the glory."*

As you await God's timing, you have the power to make wise choices and act. It is about aligning your life with the principles of love, kindness, and generosity that are often emphasized in religious teachings.

A supportive religious community can be an invaluable asset in your journey of trust and provision. The fellowship of like-minded individuals who share your faith can provide encouragement, guidance, and a sense of belonging.

Together, you can navigate the challenges you face, offering one another support and praying for each other's needs.

In practicing trust and patience, you will often find that God's blessings come in unexpected ways.

These surprises serve as reminders of His love and care. Maintaining hope is a critical component of this journey. Even in the midst of adversity, hope can be a guiding light, sustaining your belief that God is working for your good.

Romans 8:28 NIV encapsulates this idea beautifully, *"And we know that in all things God works for the good of those who love him, who have been called according to his purpose."*

It is a testament to the belief that God's provision, even in times of need, is part of His grand plan for your life. Trusting in God's provision is a journey of faith, patience, and hope that leads to a deeper connection with the divine and a profound sense of peace, even in the face of life's most daunting challenges.

Chapter 8: The Power of Gratitude and Contentment

Gratitude and contentment, when cultivated and practiced regularly, can have a profound and lasting impact on our lives.

These qualities not only help you to appreciate what you have but also to view life through a positive lens, even during challenging times.

In this chapter, I will explore how these virtues can transform our overall well-being, with a particular focus on their influence on financial prosperity.

Gratitude, which is deeply rooted in many religious and spiritual traditions, involves recognizing and acknowledging the good things in our lives, both big and small.

It can be as simple as expressing appreciation for a kind gesture or as profound as feeling grateful for our health, relationships, and opportunities. Cultivating gratitude means choosing to focus your time and attention on what you appreciate. This is key to controlling your experience and, ultimately, your well-being.[4]

I believe that contentment, on the other hand, involves being satisfied with what you have and not constantly striving for more. It is not about settling for less but rather accepting and appreciating our present circumstances while working towards our goals.

Contentment can help us avoid the trap of always chasing after more money, possessions, or status, which may lead to feelings of dissatisfaction and unhappiness.

When you practice gratitude and contentment in your financial lives, you experience greater financial well-being. Gratitude can help you to feel less anxious about money and more satisfied with what you have, while contentment can help us to avoid overspending and debt, and to make sound financial decisions.

By focusing on the good things in your life and being content with what you have, you create a positive financial mindset that will lead to long-term financial prosperity.

I recently went to a college football game at my daughter's school with a group of friends. Before the game, we set up a tent and grilled food for tailgating.

As we headed into the stadium, all the ladies locked their purses and bags in the car. The college only allowed small wallets and clear bags in the stadium.

As we approached the gates, one of the guys gave me $70 in cash for his tickets. Since I did not have a purse, I folded the bills and put them in my pants pocket.

We walked around the stadium before the game, buying drinks and snacks, looking at shirts and clear bags, and enjoying all the pregame festivities.

The game was exciting, and the home team won. We cheered and jumped up and down when the team scored.

---

[4] From "The Incredible Power of Gratitude" by Natalie Buchwald, LMHC

My daughter, being a first-year student, participated in the "freshman run" at the beginning of the game, so I took many photos with my phone pulling it in and out of my pocket during the course of the game.

After the game, when we got back to our car, I reached for the cash, but it was gone.

For just a moment, I felt a knot in my stomach; I had lost $70.

However, I decided to bless the money. I prayed that maybe it ended up in the hands of a starving college student who needed it or a janitor who was barely making ends meet.

No matter what, I released my feelings of loss and trusted that God would bless whoever had it.

I felt grateful that losing the money did not hurt me financially. Ultimately, I felt instant happiness and peace over the blessing and my trust in God.

Gratitude as a Pathway to Abundance

Gratitude is a practice that is deeply rooted in biblical teachings and is known to bring a multitude of blessings and abundance.

The Apostle Paul's words in Philippians 4:6 NIV demonstrate the importance of gratitude in our daily lives.

He wrote, *"Do not be anxious about anything, but in every situation, by prayer and petition, with thanksgiving, present your requests to God."*

This passage highlights the significance of approaching life's challenges with a thankful heart, and how gratitude can bring peace and comfort to those who seek it.

Another central theme in biblical teachings is the concept of "sowing and reaping," which is mentioned in Galatians 6:7 NIV.

The verse states, *"Do not be deceived: God can't be mocked. A man reaps what he sows."*

This idea suggests that what you put out in our lives, you get back in our lives. Cultivating gratitude in our lives is like planting the seeds of thankfulness for abundance and prosperity.

When you acknowledge the good things in your life and express gratitude for them, you attract more positivity and blessings. It is a way of opening ourselves up to receive more of what you appreciate and value.

Gratitude is not just a fleeting sentiment; it is your passport to a life rich in both spiritual fulfillment and financial abundance.

Take a moment to reflect on the extraordinary power of gratitude and how, by incorporating it deliberately into your daily existence, you open the floodgates to blessings bestowed upon you by God.

In the sacred words of Ephesians 5:20 KJV, the call to *"Give thanks always for all things unto God and the Father in the name of our Lord Jesus Christ,"* is not a distant proclamation; it is a personal directive tailored specifically for you.

This verse resonates deeply, urging you to maintain an unwavering attitude of gratitude, transcending the boundaries of perceived circumstances. It challenges you to extend thanks to God sincerely, recognizing His goodness even in the face of adversity.

Make it your mission to infuse gratitude into your every experience until it becomes second nature, an instinctive response to life's unpredictable twists and turns.

Gratitude is not just a reflection of your current blessings, but it is also a powerful thought process that helps you to believe that God will provide you with what is truly needed in your life.

When you adopt an attitude of thankfulness, it opens doors to greater abundance by creating a positive mindset and grateful spirit. The practice of gratitude is not merely a suggestion; it is a heartfelt invitation, a personal journey that transforms your perspective and fortifies your divine connection through a heart filled with thankfulness, paving the way for blessings beyond measure.

Incorporating gratitude into your daily routine can bring spiritual prosperity and financial abundance to your life.

Contentment and Its Role in Financial Well-Being

Have you ever found yourself caught up in the rat race of chasing success, defined by society's standards? In a world where success is often measured by material wealth and social status, contentment begs you to redefine your definition of success.

The Bible challenges you to redefine success, urging you to seek personal growth, meaningful connections, and a sense of purpose, along your path to accumulating wealth. It resonates with the idea that success is not just about the destination but also about the journey—the relationships you build, the personal growth you experience, and the lives you touch along the way.

In Proverbs 16:8, it is conveyed that it is better to have little gained righteously than to amass great wealth through unjust means. This verse highlights the importance of upholding righteous values and avoiding unjust practices, even when it means having to settle for lesser wealth.

By adhering to the principles of righteousness, you can enjoy a sense of moral satisfaction and contentment in life that is far more valuable than any monetary gains acquired through unjust means.

In Hebrews 13:5 NIV, it says, *"Keep your life free from love of money, and be content with what you have, for he has said, 'I will never leave you nor forsake you.'"*

You should not put your trust in money, but rather in God, who will always be with you.

1 Timothy 6:6-7 NIV also emphasizes the value of contentment, saying, *"But godliness with contentment is great gain, for we brought nothing into the world, and we can't take anything out of the world."*

In other words, you should focus on spiritual wealth rather than material wealth, as you cannot take our possessions with you when you leave this world.

The biblical encouragement to be content with what you have is not just a financial tip; it is an invitation to find peace and satisfaction in the circumstances.

All that being said, by embracing contentment you also create a fertile ground for manifesting wealth.

Psalm 37:4 reminds us that when we delight ourselves in the Lord, He grants the desires of our hearts. This is not just about material wealth but encompasses a holistic richness in life.

Personally, I have found that when I cultivate contentment and gratitude for what I have, I open myself to receiving more. Contentment acts as a magnetic force, attracting prosperity and abundance into your life.

In those moments of financial decision-making, you may have felt the tug between being responsible with the resources God has provided you and the societal pressure to amass more.

Biblically learning the secret of being content, whether faced with plenty or in times of need, is echoed in Philippians 4:11-12 NASB, *"Not that I speak from want, for I have learned to be content in whatever circumstances I am. I know how to get along with humble means, and I also know how to live in prosperity; in any and every circumstance I have learned the secret of being filled and going hungry, both of having abundance and suffering need."*

Contentment is closely tied to responsible financial stewardship. In other words, when you are content with what you have, you are more likely to manage your finances wisely, save for the future, and avoid unnecessary debt.

This responsible approach to money can lead to long-term financial well-being. As you reflect on your own contentment, you may be inspired to find joy in your journey, knowing that it is the gateway to manifesting the wealth and blessings that await you.

Attracting More by Being Thankful

Delving into the profound teachings of the Bible unveils invaluable insights into the profound connection between your actions, thoughts, and emotions and the course your life takes.

The sacred text repeatedly underscores the transformative power of your thoughts and emotions in shaping the very fabric of your reality.

A striking revelation emerges when your focus is tethered to negativity, you unwittingly draw more of it into your life.

Conversely, when you consciously direct your attention to the positive and pure aspects of existence, you magnetize a corresponding abundance.

The Bible, in its timeless wisdom, encourages you to fixate your thoughts on things that embody truth, nobility, righteousness, purity, loveliness, admiration, excellence, and praiseworthiness.

Proverbs 23:7 NIV succinctly affirms, *"For as he thinks within himself, so he is."*

This profound insight becomes a roadmap, a guide to actively create a reality that is not only positive but also abundant.

Proverbs 4:23 NIV echoes this sentiment with a powerful directive, *"Above all else, guard your heart, for everything you do flows from it."*

The emphasis lies in safeguarding the sanctuary of your inner thoughts and emotions, recognizing that they are the architects of your actions. A heart steeped in gratitude becomes a wellspring, generating a continuous flow of abundance that fuels our capacity for thankfulness.

So, in cultivating a thankful heart, you not only shield yourself from the corrosive influence of negativity but also pave the way for an ever-expanding stream of blessings to be grateful for.

As you navigate the intricate dance of thoughts and emotions, let gratitude be the melody that orchestrates a symphony of abundance in your life. You are tasked to be thankful and receive all that God has created with thankfulness.

1 Timothy 4:4 NIV reminds that, *"For everything created by God is good, and nothing is to be rejected if it is received with gratitude."*

When you adopt this attitude, you see everything as good, and you become positive and grateful in all things.

You should direct your thoughts in a way that is consistent with God's perspective. Like my story of blessing lost money, as it goes out, you have the ultimate ability to control what you think about and how you perceive things. Change your thoughts toward money and financial gain from personal gain to thoughts of building the Kingdom of God.

These verses from the Bible emphasize the profound influence of our thoughts, emotions, and actions on our lives and encourage us to focus on positivity, spiritual growth, and aligning with God's will to shape our reality in a positive way.

They also encourage you to give thanks to God in everything you do and say, acknowledging that every good thing you have comes from Him.

By cultivating a heart of gratitude, you can experience the blessings of God in your life. Gratitude and contentment are transformative forces in your life, and their impact on financial prosperity is profound.

By recognizing the biblical principles that link gratitude to abundance, understanding the role of contentment in financial well-being, and harnessing the power of thankfulness to attract more, you can shape a life filled with blessings and financial security.

Cultivating these virtues can lead to a more fulfilling and prosperous journey through life.

Chapter 9: A Giving Heart and Impactful Ministry

In a world where personal ambitions and individual pursuits often take precedence, the concept of faithful giving and impactful ministry stands out as a beacon of selflessness and purpose-driven living. It serves as a testament to the profound connection between our faith and our actions, illuminating the path to a life full of God's purpose, fulfillment, and blessings.

This chapter will explore the transformative power of supporting the community and Christian causes, the abundant blessings that flow from Christian giving, and the divine wisdom behind multiplying your wealth through God's work.

Having a giving heart is at the core of supporting Christian causes and achieving impactful ministry. This commitment is not merely an act of charity, but an act of faith, signifying our belief in God's Prosperity Plan.

The significance of our financial contributions in strengthening the body of believers and the global Christian community, emphasizes how even the smallest of gifts can have a profound impact.

When you give, you invest in the spiritual well-being of our communities and uphold the mission of Christ on Earth.

A generous heart can bring blessings to both the giver and the receiver. When you give with a grateful heart, you not only help others but also attract God's blessings and abundance.

R. G. LeTourneau was a Christian industrialist who dedicated his life to "being a businessman for God." He was hugely successful, designing and developing his own line of earth-moving equipment.

LeTourneau was the maker of nearly 300 inventions and had hundreds of patents in his lifetime. As he succeeded financially, he increased his giving to the point where he was giving 90% of his income to the Lord's work.

"I shovel out the money, and God shovels it back, but God has a bigger shovel." R. G. LeTourneau.[5]

You may be thinking that it is easy to give away most of your money when you are millionaire, but LeTourneau did not start out as a rich man.

As Christians, you are called to live out Christ's teachings in our daily lives. The Bible reminds us in 1 Peter 4:10 NASB that each of us has been blessed with unique gifts, which you should use to serve and support fellow believers.

"As each one has received a special gift, employ it in serving one another as good stewards of the multifaceted grace of God."

You are also encouraged in Matthew 5:16 NASB to let our light shine before others so that they may see our good deeds and praise God.

By giving generously and with a loving heart, you not only fulfill our Christian duty but also reflect the love of Christ to the world.

Through our actions, you bring glory to God and set an example for others to follow. Therefore, let us use our God-given gifts to serve one

---

[5] From "Money, Possession and Eternity" by Randy Alcorn

another and shine as examples of Christ's love through our giving hearts.

"A generous person will prosper; whoever refreshes others will be refreshed." Proverbs 11:25 NASB

Supporting the Community and Christian Causes

As Christians, it is our duty to support our community and Christian causes.

Our faith teaches us that the church is not just a physical structure, but a community of believers working together to spread God's love and message. By financially and spiritually supporting our local congregation, mission organizations, or Christian charities, you actively contribute to the advancement of God's kingdom on earth.

Note that this is not an argument on tithing but rather a guidance on giving.

Whether you choose to tithe, give to a charity, or support a local family in need, you are serving God according to His plan for you.

By doing so, you partake in the fulfillment of the Great Commission, which encourages us to go and make disciples of all nations.

"Then Jesus came to them and said, "All authority in heaven and on earth has been given to me. Therefore, go and make disciples of all nations, baptizing them in the name of the Father and of the Son and of the Holy Spirit, and teaching them to obey everything I have commanded you. And surely I am with you always, to the very end of the age," Matthew 28:19-20 NIV.

Essentially, you work alongside God as partners, helping to advance the growth of His kingdom.

Embracing a spirit of generosity and supporting charities that resonate with your faith is not just a good deed—it is a profoundly personal journey that beautifully reflects the teachings of the Bible and your commitment to living out your beliefs.

Hebrews 13:16 NIV gently nudges us, saying, *"And do not forget to do good and to share with others, for with such sacrifices God is pleased."*

This verse reminds us of the deep significance and pleasure found in acts of giving. In the Christian journey, we are called to mirror the compassionate actions of Jesus, as tenderly expressed in Matthew 25:40 NIV, *"Truly, I say to you, as you did it to one of the least of these my brothers, you did it to me."*

This is an invitation to embody the very essence of Christ's love.

When you extend your hands to the less fortunate, it is not just an expression of love, compassion, and selflessness; it is an active participation in a divine mandate.

By supporting charities that align with your beliefs, you become a conduit for positive change. These organizations, driven by a shared faith, work tirelessly to make a transformative impact on those in need.

In each act of kindness, you bring glory to God, fulfilling your Christian duty and reflecting the true values of your faith. This journey of giving is not a one-way street.

In sharing blessings with others, you unknowingly invite abundance into your own life. The reciprocity of generosity, as encouraged by biblical teachings, unfolds in the joy and fulfillment that quietly permeate your own existence.

Aligning your actions with your faith does not just contribute to the betterment of the world; it also adds a layer of richness and depth to your spiritual journey in ways that are both gentle and profound.

"Give, and it will be given to you. They will pour into your lap a good measure – pressed down, shaken together, and runneth over. For by your standard of measure it will be measured to you in return," Luke 6:38 NASB.

You should be mindful that when you give, you should not do so with the sole expectation of receiving material blessings in return.

Instead, the Bible teaches about the importance of giving with a selfless and open heart.

Jesus's words, 'Give, and it will be given to you,' encourage you to be generous for the sake of helping others and demonstrating God's love.

While it is true that the measure of your giving can influence the measure of blessings you receive, you should not let the desire for personal gain overshadow the genuine spirit of giving.

Giving should be an act of love and compassion, motivated by a desire to make a positive impact on the lives of others, trusting that God's blessings will come in His own way and time.

"In everything I showed you that by working hard in this manner you must help the weak and remember the words of the Lord Jesus, that He Himself said, 'It is more blessed to give than to receive,'" Acts 20:35 NASB.

The Blessings of Christian Giving

The act of Christian giving is not merely a one-way street. When you give generously and cheerfully, God promises to bless you in return.

The blessings that follow Christian giving can manifest in various ways, including financial abundance, peace, joy, and a profound sense of purpose.

Christian giving is not solely about financial contributions. It is also about cultivating a giving heart that mirrors the compassion and generosity of Christ.

God generously provides seed to the sower.

In 2 Corinthians 9:10 NIV, it says, *"Now he who supplies seed to the sower and bread for food will also supply and increase your store of seed and will enlarge the harvest of your righteousness."*

This means that when you are manifesting, meditating, and praying with a generous heart, God will guide you to find ways to give, and in return, He will bless you abundantly.

In the example given back in the goal setting section of this book, I explained that if you are setting a goal to give ten percent of your money to a Christian women's charity, and you are asking for that goal to be at least $1500, you will have $15,000.

You have increased "your store" of financial seed.

Again, careful that the place you are manifesting and praying from is for God's glory and not the personal financial gain.

In growing in your giving, you experience inner transformation, becoming a more Christlike and compassionate individual. You develop a heart that is quick to respond to the needs of others, extending love and support to those around you.

Matthew 6:20 NIV underscores this principle, *"But store up for yourselves treasures in heaven, where moths and vermin do not destroy, and where thieves do not break in and steal."*

Investing in God's work yields eternal treasures in heaven, far more valuable than any material wealth we can accumulate on Earth. These treasures include the lives touched, souls saved, and the transformation of communities and nations through the work we support.

Through your giving, you become vessels of God's love, extending His grace to a hurting world, and experiencing the profound joy of making a meaningful impact on others.

Christian giving is not a one-sided transaction, but a dynamic exchange of love, faith, and blessings – between you and God, you, and others, and between Christ and the world.

As you open your heart and wallet to the work of God, you open yourself to an abundance of blessings that flow not only into your life but into the lives of those you touch through your generosity.

Besides the spiritual blessings that come from giving, including the joy of stewardship, and the sense of purpose, you open your life to practical blessings from God.

Practical blessings, as articulated in Deuteronomy 28:1-6 NIV, are a testament to God's divine promise to those who faithfully obey Him. *"If you fully obey the Lord your God and carefully follow all his commands I give you today, the Lord your God will set you high above all the nations on earth. All these blessings will come on you and accompany you if you obey the Lord your God: You will be blessed in the city and blessed in the country. The fruit of your womb will be blessed, and the crops of your land and the young of your livestock - the calves of your herds and the lambs of your flocks. Your basket and your kneading trough will be blessed."*

These verses underscore the concept that obedience and faithfulness lead to practical blessings in every aspect of life, from your family to your livelihood.

Likewise, 2 Corinthians 9:8 NIV reaffirms the abundant nature of God's blessings. *"And God is able to bless you abundantly, so that in all things at all times, having all that you need, you will abound in every good work."*

In this verse, you see God's unwavering capacity to provide for His children, not just materially but also by equipping them to be a source of goodness and generosity to others.

These verses convey a powerful message about God's promise to bless those who obey Him and how these practical blessings enable believers to bless the world around them, thus reflecting God's grace and love.

Multiplying Your Wealth through God's Work

Christian giving is a paradox because the more you give, the more you receive. Giving generously does not decrease your wealth, but rather multiplies it.

There are spiritual laws that govern financial abundance, and aligning your resources with God's work can lead to unexpected financial growth.

The spiritual laws are the commandments and teachings of God that guide you in living a righteous and holy life.

These laws are eternal and unchanging, and they provide you with a path towards salvation and eternal life. By following these laws, you become a better steward of the wealth that has been entrusted to you.

Proverbs 11:24-25 NIV, says, *"One gives freely, yet grows all the richer; another withholds what he should give, and only suffers want. Whoever brings blessing will be enriched, and one who waters will himself be watered."*

Similarly, in Luke 6:38 NIV, it is written, *"Give, and it will be given to you. A good measure, pressed down, shaken together, and running over, will be poured into your lap. For with the measure you use, it will be measured to you."*

In other words, whatever you give you will receive, whatever amount you use, it will be the amount given to you.

God wants you to be good stewards of the wealth that has been entrusted to you, and one of the ways you can do that is by giving generously. The concept of stewardship is more than just owning something, it implies that there is a duty to manage resources responsibly and ethically.

As it says in Deuteronomy 8:18 NIV, *"But remember the LORD your God, for it is he who gives you the ability to produce wealth, and so confirms his covenant, which he swore to your ancestors, as it is today."*

It stresses the notion that wealth, be it money, possessions, or talent, is a gift from God that should be utilized in ways that respect and serve a greater purpose.

As a responsible steward of wealth, it is important to make thoughtful and conscientious choices about how you use your resources.

This means considering the impact of your financial decisions on others and the community around you. It also means promoting the idea of charitable giving, helping those in need, and ensuring that your actions are in line with God's plan.

Essentially, responsible wealth management benefits not only yourself but also your community and future generations.

Proper management of financial wealth is not just about using resources wisely, but also about using them to positively impact ministry. Rich individuals are advised to put their faith in God rather than wealth and to use their riches for charitable works, thus establishing a solid foundation for the future.

"Instruct those who are rich in this present world not to be conceited or to fix their hope on the uncertainty of riches, but on God, who richly supplies us with all things to enjoy," 1 Timothy 6:17 NASB.

Financial blessings are intended to support impactful ministry and charitable endeavors.

The Parable of the Talents (Matthew 25:14-30) in Chapter 1 of this book teaches about the responsibility to multiply the resources that God has given.

Investing your financial blessings in impactful ministries that serve others and advance God's kingdom is an important part of being a responsible steward. It allows you to witness the transformative power of financial stewardship in the realm of ministry, leading to both spiritual and material rewards.

When you give with a pure heart and a selfless spirit, you open yourself up to receive more from God, advance God's kingdom, and make a lasting impact on the community around you.

Chapter 10: Manifesting Money Through Christian Faith

Now is the time to step into a new chapter on your personal journey of manifesting money through your Christian faith.

In the pages ahead, you will delve into the intricate tapestry of your faith, your prayers, and your actions, unraveling the miracles of financial provision and testimonials of Christian prosperity.

As you navigate these principles, you will continually connect the dots between these aspects and the timeless wisdom found in biblical teachings.

I want to address now how faith is also the bedrock upon which Christian money manifestation is built. It is about trusting in God's provision and believing that He can meet your financial needs.

This chapter invites you to believe with certainty that He not only hears your prayers but is eager to meet your financial needs.

Hebrews 11:6 NIV is not just a verse; it is a guiding light on your personal journey, *"without faith, it is impossible to please God, because anyone who comes to Him must believe that He exists and that He rewards those who earnestly seek Him."*

Your steps toward Him must be filled with the conviction that He exists and will reward you as you intensely seek Him.

As a fellow believer, I encourage you to let your faith be the driving force behind your financial expectations. Embrace the unshakable certainty that, through your faith, God will manifest His prosperity in your life.

Together, let us explore the tangible and transformative power of trusting in His promises, securing a prosperous future grounded in your faith and aligned with His divine plan for your abundance.

Combining Faith, Prayer, and Action

Have you ever found yourself wondering why it seems like God does not always respond to your prayers? It is a question many of us grapple with—a common thread of human experience.

You might have heard the saying that sometimes, a "no" from God is an answer in itself.

As you journey through life, especially as a Christian seeking divine guidance, wisdom, and provision in financial matters, you may encounter moments when it feels like your prayers are met with silence.

It is essential to recognize that there could be more to the situation than meets the eye. Perhaps, the answer you seek is intricately tied to the alignment of your motives with God's greater plan.

Remember our earlier discussion about aligning with God's plan? Your faith and trust in God serve as the core of the blessings you seek.

It is not just about asking; it is about aligning your desires with His purpose for you. As the book highlighted, faith without corresponding action is lifeless, as James 2:26 NIV eloquently puts it, *"Just as the body without the spirit is dead, so also faith without works is dead."*

In the context of financial stability, it becomes apparent that taking responsible steps is crucial.

Your actions, such as budgeting wisely, making sound investments, and putting in diligent effort, become integral parts of your faith journey. It is a partnership—your faith coupled with tangible steps toward financial well-being.

So, as you navigate the intricacies of prayer and seek divine intervention in your financial matters, consider the harmony between your faith and actions. It is not merely a matter of waiting for an answer; it is about actively participating in the unfolding of God's plan for your life.

The blessings you seek may be intricately woven into the steps you take on this journey of faith.

As a Christian, you should have a strong belief in a loving God who is not only capable but also eager to provide for His children.

Philippians 4:19 NIV reinforces this, affirming that, *"And my God will meet all your needs according to the riches of His glory in Christ Jesus."*

This unwavering belief in God's abundant provision serves as the foundation for anticipating financial manifestations. Attributing your blessings to a sovereign and loving God, rather than to yourself, is key to the Christian manifestation process that fulfills God's Prosperity Plan in your life.

Psalms 35:27 NASB, *"Let them shout for joy, and rejoice, who favor my vindication; and let them say continually, 'the Lord be magnified, Who delights in the prosperity of His servant."*

Testimonies of financial miracles abound in Christian communities. These stories often involve believers facing dire financial circumstances, turning to God in prayer, and witnessing miraculous interventions.

Whether it is a sudden job opportunity, unexpected financial blessings, or debt relief, these testimonies strengthen the faith of the Christian community.

In every instance of manifesting financial wealth, give glory to God, and He will continue to prosper you.

With faith, prayer, and responsible action, you can manifest your financial goals and live a life of abundance.

"You are my God and I will praise you; you are my God and I will exalt you," Psalms 118:28 NIV.

Testimonies of Christian Prosperity

The Bible is replete with testimonies of individuals who experienced financial blessings through their faith in God. Abraham's story, which includes a faithful covenant with God, generated wealth for generations. The story of Job demonstrates how steadfast faith can lead to the restoration of wealth. And Joseph, through his unwavering trust in God, rose from slavery to a position of great authority and prosperity in Egypt. These biblical accounts serve as a source of inspiration for Christians seeking financial blessings.

Story of Abraham

Imagine being like Abraham, known as the father of faith, and experiencing a life filled with God's abundant blessings. Abraham's unwavering trust in God's promises and his obedience to His commands led to a prosperity that can inspire us all.

Let us take a closer look at his remarkable journey. In Genesis 13:2, we learn that Abraham was already blessed with incredible wealth before God even made His covenant with him.

"Now Abram was very wealthy in livestock, silver, and gold."

This verse reveals that God's favor was upon Abraham's life, showering him with material prosperity.

In Genesis 15:1, God personally assured Abraham, saying, *"Do not be afraid, Abram. I am your shield, your exceedingly great reward."*

This reassurance went beyond riches, encompassing all aspects of Abraham's life. God promised to be his abundant reward, providing not only material wealth but also spiritual and emotional blessings.

The promises did not stop there.

In Genesis 17:6, God told Abraham, *"I will make you exceedingly fruitful; and I will make nations of you, and kings shall come from you."*

This assurance of an enduring legacy implied not only future financial blessings for Abraham but also for his descendants. As the Bible later reveals, the generations that followed were indeed financially blessed, showcasing the fulfillment of God's promises.

In Genesis 24:35, Abraham's servant, speaking to Rebekah's family, testified to the abundant blessings bestowed upon his master.

"The Lord has blessed my master greatly, and he has become great; He has given him flocks and herds, silver and gold, male and female servants, and camels and donkeys."

Abraham's story is a powerful reminder of what unwavering trust in God can bring into our lives. Just as he experienced God's blessings, we too can trust in God's promises and look forward to a life filled with abundance and prosperity in all its forms.

It is a call to have faith, be obedient, and witness God's faithfulness in our own lives.

Story of Job

Job, a righteous man who faced unimaginable trials, also experienced replenished financial blessings from God.

The story of Job starts with when the fallen angel Satan approached God and tested Him asking would Job still be faithful if he lost everything he had.

God knew that Job would be faithful no matter what happened to him, and thereby gave Satan the go ahead to test Job's faith in God, as long as Satan did not lay a finger on Job.

Despite losing his wealth and possessions, Job remained faithful and trusted in God's sovereignty.

Job 42:10 NASB, *"The Lord restored the fortunes of Job when he prayed for his friends, and the Lord increased all that Job had twofold."*

God not only restored Job's financial losses but also doubled his blessings.

This story demonstrates God's faithfulness to those who remain steadfast in their faith, even amid adversity.

Job 42:12 NASB, *"The Lord blessed the latter days of Job more than his beginning; for he had fourteen thousand sheep, six thousand camels, one thousand yoke of oxen, and one thousand female donkeys."*

This verse highlights the incredible abundance that God poured upon Job after his season of suffering. It serves as a reminder that God's blessings are not limited by our circumstances, but rather, He can turn our mourning into dancing and restore us beyond what we could ever imagine.

Job 42:16 NASB, *"After this, Job lived 140 years, and saw his sons and grandsons for four generations."*

Not only did God restore Job's financial blessings, but He also granted him a long and prosperous life. God's blessings extend far beyond material wealth, encompassing every aspect of our lives.

It is a testament to God's goodness and His desire to bless His faithful servants abundantly.

Story of Joseph

Joseph's story serves as a powerful example of how unwavering faith, trust in God, and the practice of prayer can lead to financial abundance.

His story begins with him being sold into slavery by his jealous brothers.

In Genesis 39:2-4 NASB, we see Joseph's faith as he thrived even in slavery, *"The Lord was with Joseph, and he became a successful man, and he was in the house of his master, the Egyptian. His master saw that the Lord was with him and how the Lord caused all that he did to prosper in his hand. So Joseph found favor in his sight and became his personal servant; and he made him overseer over his house, and all that he owned he put in his charge."*

Despite the hardships he faced, Joseph never wavered in his faith. He trusted that God had a greater plan for his life, even when circumstances seemed bleak.

While wrongfully accused and thrown in prison, Joseph continued to seek God's guidance through prayer. God gave Joseph favor in the eyes of the chief jailer, who put him in charge of all the prisoners in the jail.

"The chief jailer did not supervise anything under Joseph's charge because the Lord was with him; and whatever he did, the Lord made him prosper," Genesis 39:23 NASB.

When Pharaoh needed someone to interpret his dreams, Joseph was brought before the Pharaoh, knowing that God had equipped him for such a task.

Genesis 41:39-40 NASB, Pharaoh says to Joseph, *"So Pharoah said to Joseph, 'Since God has informed you of all this, there is no one so discerning and wise as you are. You shall be over my house, and according to your command all my people shall do homage; only in throne I will be greater than you.'"*

Then Pharaoh took his signet ring from his finger and put it on Joseph's finger. He dressed him in robes of fine linen and put a gold chain around his neck.

Joseph went out in the land storing up all the grain to prepare for seven years of famine based on the instructions from God. God blessed this action with abundance that was so great it could not be measured. *"Thus Joseph stored up grain in great abundance like the sand of the sea, until he stopped measuring it, for it was beyond measure,"* Genesis 41:49 NASB.

Joseph's journey from slavery to financial abundance serves as a testament to the power of faith and manifesting prayer. By trusting in

God's plan, consistently praying, and acting, Joseph saw his circumstances transform drastically.

You can draw inspiration from Joseph's story and apply these principles to your own life, knowing that God is faithful to provide for those who seek Him wholeheartedly.

As you embrace these biblical teachings, may you too experience financial abundance and blessings beyond measure.

Modern Testimonies

It is truly inspiring to witness the countless testimonies of financial prosperity that believers in contemporary Christianity have experienced through their faith.

These stories serve as a powerful reminder of the enduring power of faith and the unwavering trust in God's providence. From overcoming overwhelming debt to starting successful businesses, these modern-day accounts of financial manifestation are shared within church communities, on social media platforms, and through various forms of media.

They serve as a testament to the incredible ways in which God can intervene and provide for His children in times of need. Just a simple internet search for Christian manifestation miracles will reveal a plethora of stories that fill the screen.

These testimonies, including my own experience shared earlier in this book, are a source of hope and encouragement for those facing financial challenges.

John D. Rockefeller

John D. Rockefeller, one of the world's wealthiest individuals, was known for embodying the Christian principle of generosity, having donated a remarkable $550 million during his lifetime.

In terms of his Christian faith, Rockefeller's commitment was unwavering. He made it a daily practice to read the Bible, attended prayer meetings twice a week, and even led his own Bible study sessions with his wife.

His dedication extended to tithing, observing the Sabbath for rest, and consistently allocating a substantial portion of his wealth to charitable causes.

In a letter to his son in 1924, he revealed his approach to giving money, stating, "...from the very outset of my financial journey, stretching back to my childhood, I began the practice of giving, and I escalated these contributions in tandem with my increasing income."

Evidently, his philosophy of philanthropy was deeply rooted in biblical principles. He wholeheartedly embraced the biblical wisdom encapsulated in Luke 6:38 NIV, which advises, *"Give, and it will be given to you. A good measure, pressed down, shaken together, and running over, will be poured into your lap. For with the measure you use, it will be measured to you."*

Through his faith, prayer, generosity, and action Rockefeller was given financial abundance from God that was immeasurable.

Jay Cooke

Jay Cooke's contribution to American society is indelibly marked by his pivotal role in shaping the nation's financial landscape.

As a visionary financier and banker, Cooke is considered America's first investment banker and was one of the richest men in the 19th century.

His impact extended beyond mere financial success; Cooke's philanthropic endeavors, including his support for education and the founding of Swarthmore College, underscored his commitment to societal betterment.

He also donated vast amounts of money to Episcopalian charities and financed the construction of many churches.

Jay Cooke's testimony stands as a testament to the miraculous workings of God in the realm of abundance. With steadfast faith and a profound link to Christian values, Cooke's contemporary account stands as a source of inspiration for those who believe.

It illustrates that by embracing faith, practicing generosity, and aligning with divine principles, one can witness the extraordinary intervention of God in the realm of financial prosperity.

His story echoes the timeless truth that faith, coupled with obedience and trust, can unlock doors to prosperity beyond human comprehension.

J. Howard Pew

J. Howard Pew, a prominent industrialist and philanthropist in the 20th century, stands as a contemporary testament to the intersection of faith and God's provision.

As the leader of Sun Oil Company (Sunoco) and a devout Christian, Pew not only achieved considerable success in the business world but also demonstrated a remarkable generosity fueled by his faith.

His philanthropic endeavors included substantial contributions to educational institutions like the University of Pennsylvania, backing conservative causes, and notably, founding Christianity Today Magazine.

By establishing this influential publication, Pew aimed to promote Christian values and foster meaningful discussions on matters of faith.

Pew's financial support extended to organizations promoting Christian values and religious freedom. Through his benevolence, Pew showcased the substantial financial outcomes of a life grounded in faith, illustrating that God's provision could be channeled into transformative acts of kindness and support for the betterment of society.

It is worth noting that Pew's conservative values and principles influenced his business decisions, and he was known for integrating his Christian faith into both his personal life and the management of Sun Oil Company.

This intersection of business success, personal values, and faith ultimately shaped his legacy as an influential figure in both the business and philanthropic spheres.

David Green

David Green, the billionaire proprietor of Hobby Lobby, is another contemporary testimony to the profound interplay of faith, generosity, and financial prosperity.

Grounded in Christian beliefs, Green authentically weaves his devotion into the very fabric of Hobby Lobby's accomplishments. His open acknowledgment of the impact of his Christian beliefs on business practices reflects a genuine commitment to integrating religious values into the core of the company.

Green has openly declared that both his personal success and the triumphs of Hobby Lobby are manifestations of God's blessings.

This deep trust in God's guidance has become a hallmark of Green's journey, evident not only in the strategic closure of stores on Sundays but also in fostering a workplace environment infused with positivity and faith.

Beyond the business realm, Green's philanthropy, marked by significant donations to educational institutions and the establishment of the Museum of the Bible, exemplifies a profound dedication to giving back.

David Green's life unfolds as a compelling testimony, showcasing how aligning one's business endeavors with faith and embodying generosity can lead to both material success and a powerful testament to the workings of God's providence.

The manifestation of money through Christian faith involves a beautiful interplay of unwavering trust in God, fervent prayer, and responsible action.

Believers place their faith in a loving and providential God, while seeking His guidance and blessings in their financial endeavors. It is important to remember that financial manifestation is not about a "get rich quick" scheme or a guarantee of material wealth.

Rather, it is about aligning our hearts and actions with God's will and trusting Him to provide for our needs.

As you continue your own financial journey, I encourage you to hold onto your faith tightly. Seek God's guidance, pray fervently, and take responsible action in your financial decisions. Trust that He is with you every step of the way, ready to provide for your needs according to His perfect timing and plan.

May the testimonies of Christian prosperity and the miracles of financial provision serve as a reminder of the incredible potency of faith in the financial realm.

May they inspire you to continue placing your trust in God, knowing that He is faithful to His promises.

Keep believing, keep praying, and keep taking responsible action, for God's blessings are abundant and His love for you is unwavering.

Conclusion

When comparing Christian testimonies of financial prosperity with those in the context of the law of attraction, it is crucial to acknowledge the foundational contrast in their underlying worldviews.

Both systems underscore the importance of positive thinking and unwavering belief, yet Christians attribute their prosperity to God's grace and providence, prioritizing humility and gratitude.

At the outset of this book, I aimed to demonstrate that manifestation is inherently rooted in biblical teachings, and the principles associated with the modern concept of the Law of Attraction can be found throughout the Bible.

However, there exists one significant variance: Christian Manifestation is grounded in a deep connection with God. It is not driven by self-serving motives or personal gain; rather, its purpose is to glorify God, advance His Kingdom, and generate wealth for future generations.

Embracing God's Abundant Blessings

When embracing God's abundant blessings, it is paramount that you ground your faith in His promises and unwavering trust in His providence.

As the book of Proverbs 3:5-6 NIV reminds us, *"Trust in the LORD with all your heart, and do not lean on your own understanding. In all your ways acknowledge him, and he will make straight your paths."*

By leaning on His guidance and steadfast love, you allow God to bestow His abundant blessings upon you, as it states in Philippians 4:19 NIV, *"And my God will supply every need of yours according to his riches in glory in Christ Jesus."*

You should wholeheartedly place your trust in Him, you can confidently embrace the abundance of His blessings, knowing that they flow from a loving and faithful God.

Embracing God's abundance is also an act of profound belief and unwavering faith in His promises.

Romans 15:13 NIV reminds you, *"May the God of hope fill you with all joy and peace in believing, so that by the power of the Holy Spirit you may abound in hope."*

This abounding hope and belief in God's abundant blessings are further emphasized in Mark 9:23 NIV, which states, *"All things are possible for one who believes."*

Through your steadfast faith, you open yourself to receive the boundless gifts and abundance that God has prepared for you.

Ephesians 3:20 NIV, *"Now to him who is able to do immeasurably more than all we ask or imagine, according to his power that is at work within us."*

Thus, in embracing God's abundance, your belief and faith pave the way for His divine blessings to flow into your life, reminding you of His limitless grace and love.

Walking in Faith and Financial Prosperity

Walking in faith is a key component of experiencing financial prosperity within the context of Christian Manifestation. It is not merely about superficial belief but a deep and unwavering trust in God's plan for your financial well-being.

Just as the book of Hebrews 11:1 NIV states, *"Now faith is the assurance of things hoped for, the conviction of things not seen."*

When you walk in faith, you demonstrate your conviction that God's promises, including financial blessings, are real and attainable. This trust in God's provision leads to an enduring sense of peace and confidence, even in the face of financial challenges.

Financial prosperity, when guided by faith, is not a guarantee of endless riches, but it offers the assurance that God will provide for your needs and equip you to fulfill your purpose.

As you embark on your journey of financial prosperity through faith, remember the words of Psalm 37:25 NIV, *"I have been young, and now am old, yet I have not seen the righteous forsaken nor his children begging for bread."*

This trust in God's faithfulness empowers you to take steps of financial responsibility while keeping faith at the core of your financial decisions.

A Lifelong Journey of Manifesting Money with the Bible

Starting your personal journey to manifesting money using the wisdom of the Bible is like making a lifelong vow between God and yourself.

It is a commitment to blend your money goals with what God teaches in the Bible. Think of it as a journey of always growing, learning, and changing as you bring the Bible's wisdom into how you handle money.

Just like Proverbs 16:3 NIV says, *"Commit to the Lord whatever you do, and He will establish your plans."*

This means your money plans are rooted in what God advises.

However, this journey extends beyond personal gain; it is about contributing to the greater good.

Aligning your financial pursuits with the principles of the Bible becomes a means of spreading God's message and ensuring the well-being of future generations.

Reflect on 2 Corinthians 9:10 NIV, which likens God's provision to a farmer receiving seeds for cultivation and bread for sustenance. *"God gives seed to the farmer and bread for food. He will also give you seed and multiply it. In the end, you will have everything you need and more to give."*

In following these teachings, you not only secure your own prosperity but also cultivate abundance to share with others.

To sum it up, getting rich and successful the Bible's way is not a quick fix. It is a promise to keep on having faith, trusting in God, and using the Bible's teachings in your money decisions.

By choosing to walk in faith and making a lifelong effort to make money with the Bible, you not only make sure your money is secure but also match your goals with what God desires.

This brings glory to Him and leaves a legacy of blessings for future generations.

May your money journey be guided by strong faith, trusting in God's promises, and having a deep connection with Him.

Enjoy all the good things He gives, and may you see financial success according to His plan.

Bible References

Genesis 15:1: "Do not be afraid, Abram. I am your shield, your exceedingly great reward."

Genesis 17:6: "I will make you exceedingly fruitful; and I will make nations of you, and kings shall come from you."

Genesis 24:35: "The Lord has blessed my master greatly, and he has become great; He has given him flocks and herds, silver and gold, male and female servants, and camels and donkeys."

Genesis 39:2-4 NASB: "The Lord was with Joseph, and he became a successful man, and he was in the house of his master, the Egyptian. His master saw that the Lord was with him and how the Lord caused all that he did to prosper in his hand. So Joseph found favor in his sight and became his personal servant; and he made him overseer over his house, and all that he owned he put in his charge."

Genesis 39:23 NASB: "The chief jailer did not supervise anything under Joseph's charge because the Lord was with him; and whatever he did, the Lord made him prosper."

Genesis 41:39-40 NASB: "So Pharoah said to Joseph, 'Since God has informed you of all this, there is no one so discerning and wise as you are.

You shall be over my house, and according to your command all my people shall do homage; only in throne I will be greater than you.'"

Genesis 41:49 NASB: "Thus Joseph stored up grain in great abundance like the sand of the sea, until he stopped measuring it, for it was beyond measure."

Deuteronomy 8:18 NIV: "But remember the LORD your God, for it is he who gives you the ability to produce wealth, and so confirms his covenant, which he swore to your ancestors, as it is today."

Deuteronomy 16:17 NIV: "Every man shall give as he is able, according to the blessing of the Lord your God which He has given you."

Deuteronomy 28:1-6 NIV: "If you fully obey the Lord your God and carefully follow all his commands I give you today, the Lord your God will set you high above all the nations on earth. All these blessings will come on you and accompany you if you obey the Lord your God: You will be blessed in the city and blessed in the country. The fruit of your womb will be blessed, and the crops of your land and the young of your livestock - the calves of your herds and the lambs of your flocks. Your basket and your kneading trough will be blessed."

Deuteronomy 31:6 NIV: "Be strong and courageous. Do not be afraid or terrified because of them, for the Lord your God goes with you; He will never leave you nor forsake you."

Job 42:10 NASB: "The Lord restored the fortunes of Job when he prayed for his friends, and the Lord increased all that Job had twofold."

Job 42:12 NASB: "The Lord blessed the latter days of Job more than his beginning; for he had fourteen thousand sheep, six thousand camels, one thousand yoke of oxen, and one thousand female donkeys."

Job 42:16 NASB: "After this, Job lived 140 years, and saw his sons and grandsons for four generations."

Psalms 1:2-3 NASB: "But his delight is in the law of the Lord, And in His law he meditates day and night. He will be like a tree firmly planted by streams of water, which yields its fruit in its season and its leaf does not wither; And in whatever he does, he prospers."

Psalms 20:4 NIV: "May he give you the desire of your heart and make all your plans succeed."

Psalm 23:1 NIV: "The Lord is my shepherd, I lack nothing."

Psalms 24:1 NIV: "The earth is the Lord's, and everything in it, the world, and all who live in it."

Psalms 27:14 NIV: "Wait for the Lord; be strong and take heart and wait for the Lord." This is a powerful instruction from God to wait on Him and his timing.

Psalms 32:8 NIV: "I will instruct you and teach you in the way you should go; I will counsel you with my loving eye on you,"

Psalms 35:27 NASB: "Let them shout for joy, and rejoice, who favor my vindication; and let them say continually, 'the Lord be magnified, Who delights in the prosperity of His servant."

Psalms 37:3-4 NASB: "Trust in the Lord and do good; Dwell in the land and cultivate faithfulness. Delight yourself in the Lord; and He will give you the desires of your heart."

Psalms 37:3-5 NIV: "Trust in the Lord and do good; dwell in the land and enjoy safe pasture. Take delight in the Lord, and he will give you the desires of your heart. Commit your way to the Lord; trust in him and he will do this."

Psalm 37:25 NIV: "I have been young, and now am old, yet I have not seen the righteous forsaken nor his children begging for bread."

Psalms 46:1 NIV: "God is our refuge and strength, an ever-present help in trouble."

Psalms 56:3-4 NIV: "When I am afraid, I put my trust in you. In God, whose word I praise – in God I trust and am not afraid."

Psalms 65:11 NIV: "You crown the year with your bounty and your carts overflow with abundance."

Psalms 62:8 NIV: "Trust in him at all times, you people; pour out your hearts to him, for God is our refuge."

Psalms 100:4-5: "Enter His gates with thanksgiving and his courts with praise; give thanks to Him and praise His name. For the Lord is good and His love endures forever; His faithfulness continues through all generations."

Psalms 118:28 NIV: "You are my God and I will praise you; you are my God and I will exalt you."

Psalms 119:105 NIV: "Your word is a lamp for my feet, a light on my path."

Proverbs 3:3-4 NASB: "Do not let kindness and truth leave you; Bind them around your neck, Write them on the tablet of your heart. So you will find favor and good repute in the sight of God and man."

Proverbs 3:5-6 NIV: "Trust in the Lord with all your heart and lean not on your own understanding; in all your ways submit to Him, and He will make your paths straight."

Proverbs 3:9-10 NIV: "Honor the Lord with your wealth, with the first fruits of all your crops; then your barns will be filled to overflowing, and your vats will brim over with new wine."

Proverbs 4:23 NIV: "Above all else, guard your heart, for everything you do flows from it."

Proverbs 6:6-8 NIV: "Go to the ant, you sluggard; consider its ways and be wise! It has no commander, no overseer or ruler, yet it stores its provisions in summer and gathers its food at harvest."

Proverbs 10:4 NIV: "Lazy hands make for poverty, but diligent hands bring wealth."

Proverbs 10:22 NIV: "The blessing of the Lord brings wealth, without painful toil for it."

Proverbs 11:1 NIV: "The Lord detests dishonest scales, but accurate weights find favor with him."

Proverbs 11:24-25 NIV: "One gives freely, yet grows all the richer; another withholds what he should give, and only suffers want. Whoever brings blessing will be enriched, and one who waters will himself be watered."

Proverbs 13:11 NIV: "Dishonest money dwindles away, but whoever gathers money little by little makes it grow."

Proverbs 13:22 NIV: "A good person leaves an inheritance for their children's children, but a sinner's wealth is stored up for the righteous."

Proverbs 15:22 NIV: "Plans fail for lack of counsel, but with many advisers they succeed."

Proverbs 16:3 NIV: "Commit to the Lord whatever you do, and He will establish your plans."

Proverbs 16:9 NIV: "In their hearts humans plan their course, but the Lord establishes their steps."

Proverbs 16:11 NIV: "Honest scales and balances belong to the Lord; all the weights in the bag are of his making."

Proverbs 16:16 NASB: "How much better it is to get wisdom than gold! And to get understanding is to be chosen above silver."

Proverbs 16:20 NIV: "Whoever gives heed to instruction prospers, and blessed is the one who trusts in the Lord."

Proverbs 17:18 NIV: "One who has no sense shakes hands in pledge and puts up security for a neighbor."

Proverbs 18:21 NIV: "the tongue has the power of life and death."

Proverbs 19:17 NIV: "Whoever is kind to the poor lends to the Lord, and he will reward them for what they have done."

Proverbs 19:17 NASB: "One who is gracious to a poor man lends to the Lord, And He will repay him for his good deed."

Proverbs 20:21 NIV: "An inheritance claimed too soon will not be blessed at the end."

Proverbs 21:5 NIV: "The plans of the diligent lead to profit as surely as haste leads to poverty."

Proverbs 22:1 NIV: "A good name is more desirable than great riches; to be esteemed is better than silver or gold."

Proverbs 22:7 NIV: "The rich rule over the poor, and the borrower is slave to the lender."

Proverbs 23:7 KJV: "For as he thinketh in his heart, so is he."

Proverbs 23:7 NIV: "For as he thinks within himself, so he is."

Proverbs 28:20 NIV: "A faithful person will be richly blessed, but one eager to get rich will not go unpunished."

Proverbs 28:22 NIV: "The stingy are eager to get rich and are unaware that poverty awaits them."

Proverbs 28:27 NIV: "Those who give to the poor will lack nothing, but those who close their eyes to them receive many curses."

Ecclesiastes 3:1 NIV: "There is a time for everything and a season for every activity under the heavens."

Ecclesiastes 5:10 NASB: "He who loves money will not be satisfied with money, nor he who loves abundance with its income. This too is vanity."

Ecclesiastes 5:19 NASB: "Furthermore, as for every man to whom God has given riches and wealth, He has also empowered him to eat from them and to receive his reward and rejoice in his labor; this is the gift from God."

Ecclesiastes 11:2 NIV: "Invest in seven ventures, yes, in eight; you do not know what disaster may come upon the land."

Ecclesiastes 11:4 NIV: "Whoever watches the wind will not plant; whoever looks at the clouds will not reap."

Isaiah 30:21 NIV: "Whether you turn to the right or to the left, your ears will hear a voice behind you, saying, 'This is the way; walk in it."

Isaiah 40:31 NIV: "But those who hope in the Lord will renew their strength. They will soar on wings like eagles; they will run and not grow weary, they will walk and not be faint."

Isaiah 41:10 NIV: "So do not fear, for I am with you; do not be dismayed, for I am your God. I will strengthen you and help you; I will uphold you with my righteous right hand."

Isaiah 45:5-6 NIV: "I am the Lord, and there is no other; apart from me there is no God. I will strengthen you, though you have not acknowledged me, so that from the rising of the sun to the place of its setting people may know there is none besides me. I am the Lord, and there is no other."

Jeremiah 17:7-8 NIV: "But blessed is the one who trusts in the Lord, whose confidence is in him. They will be like a tree planted by the water that sends out its roots by the stream. It does not fear when heat comes; its leaves are always green. It has no worries in a year of drought and never fails to bear fruit."

Jeremiah 29:5 NASB: "Build houses and live in them; and plant gardens and eat their produce."

Jeremiah 29:11 NIV: "For I know the plans I have for you, declares the Lord, plans to prosper you and not to harm you, plans to give you hope and a future."

Jeremiah 29:14 NASB: "You will seek Me and find Me when you search for Me with all your heart. I will be found by you, declares the Lord."

Micah 6:8 NIV: "He has shown you, O mortal, what is good. And what does the Lord require of you? To act justly and to love mercy and to walk humbly with your God."

Malachi 3:10 KJV: "Bring ye all the tithes into the storehouse, that there may be meat in mine house, and prove me now herewith, saith the Lord of hosts, if I will not open you the windows of heaven, and pour you out a blessing, that there shall not be room enough to receive it."

Malachi 3:10-11 NASB: "Bring the whole tithe into the storehouse, so that there may be food in My house, and test Me now in this," says the Lord of hosts, "if I will not open for you the windows of heaven and pour out for you a blessing until it overflows. Then I will rebuke the devourer for you, so that it will not destroy the fruits of the ground; nor will your vine in the field cast its grapes,' says the Lord of hosts."

Matthew 3:16-17 NIV: "As soon as Jesus was baptized, he went up out of the water. At that moment heaven was opened, and he saw the Spirit of God descending like a dove and alighting on him. And a voice from heaven said, 'This is my Son, whom I love; with him I am well pleased."

Matthew 5:3 NIV, "Blessed are the poor in spirit, for theirs is the kingdom of heaven."

Matthew 5:16 NIV: "In the same way, let your light shine before others, that they may see your good deeds and glorify your Father in heaven."

Matthew 6:20 NIV: "But store up for yourselves treasures in heaven, where moths and vermin do not destroy, and where thieves do not break in and steal."

Matthew 6:24 NIV: "No one can serve two masters. Either you will hate the one and love the other, or you will be devoted to the one and despise the other. You can't serve both God and money."

Matthew 6:25-27 NIV: "Therefore I tell you, do not worry about your life, what you will eat or drink; or about your body, what you will wear. Is not life more than food, and the body more than clothes? Look at the birds of the air; they do not sow or reap or store away in barns, and yet your heavenly Father feeds them. Are you not much more valuable than they?"

Matthew 6:33 NIV: "But seek first his kingdom and his righteousness, and all these things will be given to you as well."

Matthew 7:1 NASB: "Do not judge so that you will not be judged."

Matthew 7:11 NIV: "If you, then, though you are evil, know how to give good gifts to your children, how much more will your Father in heaven give good gifts to those who ask Him!"

Matthew 7:12 NASB: "In everything, therefore, treat people the same way you want them to treat you, for this is the Law and the Prophets."

Matthew 10:8 NIV: "Freely you have received; freely give."

Matthew 13:11-12 NIV: "He replied, 'Because the knowledge of the secrets of the kingdom of heaven has been given to you, but not to them. Whoever has will be given more, and they will have an abundance.'"

Matthew 18:20 NASB: "For where two or three have gathered together in My name, I am there in their midst."

Matthew 21:22 NIV: "If you believe, you will receive whatever you ask for in prayer."

Matthew 25:29 NASB: "For to everyone who has, more shall be given, and he will have an abundance; but from the one who does not have, even what he does have shall be taken away."

Matthew 25:35-36 NASB: "For I was hungry, and you gave Me something to eat; I was thirsty, and you gave Me something to drink; I was a stranger, and you invited Me in; naked, and you clothed Me; I was sick, and you visited Me; I was in prison, and you came to Me."

Matthew 25:40 NASB: "The King will answer and say to them, 'Truly I say to you, to the extent that you did it to one of these brothers of Mine, even the least of them, you did it to Me.'"

Matthew 25:40 NIV: "Truly, I say to you, as you did it to one of the least of these my brothers, you did it to me."

Matthew 28:19-20 NIV: "Then Jesus came to them and said, "All authority in heaven and on earth has been given to me. Therefore, go and make disciples of all nations, baptizing them in the name of the Father and of the Son and of the Holy Spirit, and teaching them to obey everything I have commanded you. And surely I am with you always, to the very end of the age."

Mark 9:23 NIV: "All things are possible for one who believes."

Mark 11:24 NIV: "Therefore I tell you, whatever you ask for in prayer, believe that you have received it, and it will be yours."

Luke 6:38 NASB: "Give, and it will be given to you. They will pour into your lap a good measure – pressed down, shaken together, and runneth over. For by your standard of measure it will be measured to you in return."

Luke 6:38 NIV: "Give, and it will be given to you. A good measure, pressed down, shaken together and running over, will be poured into your lap. For with the measure you use, it will be measured to you."

Luke 8:17 KJV: "For nothing is secret, that shall not be made manifest; neither any thing hid, that shall not be known or come abroad."

Luke 12:15 NIV: "Watch out! Be on your guard against all kinds of greed; life does not consist in an abundance of possessions."

Luke 18:27 NASB: "The things that are impossible with people are possible with God,"

John 2:11: "This beginning of His signs Jesus did in Cana of Galilee, and manifested His glory, and His disciples believed in Him."

John 3:16 KJV: "For God so loved the world, he gave his only begotten Son, that whosoever believes in him shall not perish but have everlasting life."

John 3:21 NASB: "But he who practices the truth comes to the Light, so that his deeds may be manifested as having been wrought in God."

John 13:34-35 NIV" "A new command I give you: Love one another. As I have loved you, so you must love one another. By this everyone will know that you are my disciples if you love one another."

John 15:7 NASB: "If you abide in Me, and My words abide in you, ask whatever you wish, and it will be done for you."

John 15:16 NIV: "You did not choose me, but I chose you and appointed you so that you might go and bear fruit – fruit that will last – and so that whatever you ask in my name the Father will give you."

John 21:1 NASB: "After these things Jesus manifested Himself again to the disciples at the Sea of Tiberias"

Acts 20:35 NASB: "In everything I showed you that by working hard in this manner you must help the weak and remember the words of the Lord Jesus, that He Himself said, 'It is more blessed to give than to receive.'"

Acts 20:35 NIV: "In everything I did, I showed you that by this kind of hard work we must help the weak, remembering the words the Lord himself said: 'it is more blessed to give than to receive.'"

Romans 8:28 NIV: "And we know that in all things God works for the good of those who love him, who have been called according to his purpose."

Romans 8:32 NIV: "He who did not spare His own Son, but gave Him up for us all – how will He not also, along with Him, graciously give us all things?"

Romans 12:2 NIV: "Do not conform to the pattern of this world, but be transformed by the renewing of your mind."

Romans 12:2 NASB: "And do not be conformed to this world, but be transformed by the renewing of your mind, so that you may prove what the will of God is, that which is good and acceptable and perfect."

Romans 13:7-8 NIV: "Give to everyone what you owe them: If you owe taxes, pay taxes; if revenue, then revenue; if respect, then respect; if honor, then honor. Let no debt remain outstanding, except the continuing debt to love one another, for whoever loves others has fulfilled the law."

Romans 15:13 NIV: "May the God of hope fill you with all joy and peace as you trust in him, so that you may overflow with hope by the power of the Holy Spirit."

1 Corinthians 4:2 NIV: "Now it is required that those who have been given a trust must prove faithful."

1 Corinthians 16:2 NIV: "On the first day of every week, each one of you should set aside a sum of money in keeping with your income, saving it up, so that when I come no collections will have to be made."

2 Corinthians 2:14 NASB: "But thanks be to God, who always leads us in triumph in Christ, and manifests through us the sweet aroma of the knowledge of Him in every place."

2 Corinthians 5:7 NIV: "For we live by faith, not by sight."

2 Corinthians 9:6-7 NASB: "The point is this: whoever sows sparingly will also reap sparingly, and whoever sows bountifully will also reap bountifully. Each one must give as he has decided in his heart, not reluctantly or under compulsion, for God loves a cheerful giver."

2 Corinthians 9:8 NIV: "And God is able to bless you abundantly, so that in all things at all times, having all that you need, you will abound in every good work."

2 Corinthians 9:10 NIV: "Now he who supplies seed to the sower and bread for food will also supply and increase your store of seed and will enlarge the harvest of your righteousness."

Galatians 5:14 NASB: "For the whole Law is fulfilled in one word, in the statement, 'You shall love your neighbor as yourself.'"

Galatians 6:7 NIV: "Do not be deceived: God can't be mocked. A man reaps what he sows."

Ephesians 3:20 NASB: "Now to Him who is able to do far more abundantly beyond all that we ask or think, according to the power that works within us, to Him be the glory."

Ephesians 3:20 NIV: "Now to him who is able to do immeasurably more than all we ask or imagine, according to his power that is at work within us."

Ephesians 4:31-32 NIV: "Get rid of all bitterness, rage, and anger, brawling and slander, along with every form of malice. Be kind and compassionate to one another, forgiving each other, just as in Christ God forgave you."

Ephesians 5:20 KJV: "Give thanks always for all things unto God and the Father in the name of our Lord Jesus Christ."

Philippians 4:6-7 NIV: "Do not be anxious about anything, but in every situation, by prayer and petition, with thanksgiving, present your requests to God. And the peace of God, which transcends all understanding, will guard your hearts and your minds in Christ Jesus."

Philippians 4:8 NIV: "Finally, brothers and sisters, whatever is true, whatever is noble, whatever is right, whatever is pure, whatever is lovely, whatever is admirable—if anything is excellent or praiseworthy—think about such things."

Philippians 4:11-12 NASB: "Not that I speak from want, for I have learned to be content in whatever circumstances I am. I know how to get along with humble means, and I also know how to live in prosperity; in any and every circumstance I have learned the secret of being filled and going hungry, both of having abundance and suffering need."

Philippians 4:13 NIV: "I can do all this through him who gives me strength."

Philippians 4:19 NIV: "And my God will meet all your needs according to the riches of His glory in Christ Jesus."

Colossians 2:8 NIV: "See to it that no one takes you captive through hollow and deceptive philosophy, which depends on human tradition and the elemental spiritual forces of this world rather than on Christ."

Colossians 3:2 NASB: "Set your mind on the things above, not on the things that are on earth."

Colossians 3:8-10 NIV: "But now you must rid yourselves of all such things as these: anger, rage, malice, slander, and filthy language from your lips. Do not lie to each other, since you have taken off your old self with its practices and have put on the new self, which is being renewed in knowledge in the image of its Creator."

Colossians 3:16 NASB: "Let the word of Christ richly dwell within you, with all wisdom teaching and admonishing one another with psalms and hymns and spiritual songs, singing with thankfulness in your hearts to God."

Colossians 3:17 NASB: "Whatever you do in word or deed, do all in the name of Lord Jesus, giving thanks through Him to God the Father."

Colossians 3:23-24 NIV: "Whatever you do, work at it with all your heart, as working for the Lord, not for human masters, since you know that you will receive an inheritance for the Lord as a reward. It is the Lord Christ you are serving."

1 Thessalonians 5:16-18 NIV: "Rejoice always, pray continually, give thanks in all circumstances; for this is God's will for you in Christ Jesus."

2 Thessalonians 3:10 NIV: "For even when we were with you, we gave you this rule: 'The one who is unwilling to work shall not eat."

1 Timothy 4:4 NIV: "For everything created by God is good, and nothing is to be rejected if it is received with gratitude."

1 Timothy 5:8 NASB: "But if anyone does not provide for his own, and especially for those of his household, he as denied the faith and is worse than an unbeliever."

1 Timothy 6:6-8 NIV: "But godliness with contentment is great gain. For we brought nothing into the world, and we can take nothing out of it. But if we have food and clothing, we will be content with that."

1 Timothy 6:9-10 NIV: "Those who want to get rich fall into temptation and a trap and into many foolish and harmful desires that plunge people into ruin and destruction. For the love of money is a root of all kinds of evil. Some people, eager for money, have wandered from the faith and pierced themselves with many griefs."

1 Timothy 6:17-18 NASB: "Instruct those who are rich in this present world not to be conceited or to set their hope on the uncertainty of riches, but on God, who richly supplies us with all things to enjoy. Instruct them to do good, to be rich in good works, to be generous and ready to share, storing up for themselves the treasure of a good foundation for the future, so that they may take hold of that which is truly life."

2 Timothy 3:16-17 NASB: "All Scripture is inspired by God and profitable for teaching, for reproof, for correction, for training in righteousness; so that the man of God may be adequate, equipped for every good work,"

Hebrews 6:12 NIV: "We do not want you to become lazy, but to imitate those who through faith and patience inherit what has been promised."

Hebrews 11:1 NIV: "Now faith is confidence in what we hope for and assurance about what we do not see."

Hebrews 11:6 NIV: "without faith, it is impossible to please God, because anyone who comes to Him must believe that He exists and that He rewards those who earnestly seek Him."

Hebrews 12:11 NIV: "No discipline seems pleasant at the time, but painful. Later on, however, it produces a harvest of righteousness and peace for those who have been trained by it."

Hebrews 13:5 NIV: "Keep your lives free from the love of money and be content with what you have, because God has said, 'Never will I leave you; never will I forsake you.'"

Hebrews 13:16 NIV: "And do not forget to do good and to share with others, for with such sacrifices God is pleased."

James 1:5-6 NIV: "If any of you lacks wisdom, you should ask God, who gives generously to all without finding fault, and it will be given to you. But when you ask, you must believe and not doubt, because the one who doubts is like a wave of the sea, blown and tossed by the wind."

James 2:26 NIV: "Just as the body without the spirit is dead, so also faith without works is dead."

James 3:17- 18 NASB: "But the wisdom from above is first pure, then peaceable, gentle, reasonable, full of mercy and good fruits, unwavering, without hypocrisy. And the seed whose fruit is righteousness is sown in peace by those who make peace."

James 4:3 NIV warns, "When you ask, you do not receive, because you ask with wrong motives, that you may spend what you get on your pleasures."

James 4:13-15 NASB: "Come now, you who say, 'Today or tomorrow we will go to such and such a city, and spend a year there and engage in business and make a profit.' Yet you do not know what your life will be like tomorrow. You are just a vapor that appears for a little while and then vanishes away. Instead, you ought to say, 'If the Lord wills, we will live and also do this or that.'"

1 John 5:14-15 NIV: "This is the confidence we have in approaching God: that if we ask anything according to His will, He hears us. And if we know that he hears us – whatever we ask – we know that we have what we asked of Him."

Debt Snowball Tracker

MONTH OF

CREDITOR

ACCOUNT #

AMOUNT

DUE DATE

INTEREST RATE

GOAL PAYOFF DATE

MINIMUM PAYMENT

DATE	ACCOUNT	BALANCE	NOTES

VISUAL PAYOFF PROGRESS

$ — 100%
$ — 95%
$ — 90%
$ — 85%
$ — 80%
$ — 75%
$ — 70%
$ — 65%
$ — 60%
$ — 55%
$ — 50%
$ — 45%
$ — 40%
$ — 35%
$ — 30%
$ — 25%
$ — 20%
$ — 15%
$ — 10%
$ — 5%
$ — 0%